THE WAY
TO LOVE

THE WAY
TO LOVE

THE LAST MEDITATIONS OF
ANTHONY DE MELLO

DOUBLEDAY

NEW YORK   LONDON   TORONTO   SYDNEY   AUCKLAND

PUBLISHED BY DOUBLEDAY
a division of Bantam Doubleday Dell Publishing Group, Inc.
666 Fifth Avenue, New York, New York 10103

DOUBLEDAY and the portrayal of an anchor with a dolphin are
trademarks of Doubleday, a division of Bantam Doubleday Dell
Publishing Group, Inc.

The Way to Love was originally published as *Call to Love* in
India in 1991 by Gujarat Sahitya Prakash. This Doubleday
edition published October 1992.

Imprimi potest: Lisbert D'Souza, S.J.
                   Provincial of Bombay
                   March 11, 1991
Imprimatur: +Stanislaus Fernandes, S.J.
                   Bishop of Ahmedabad
                   March 18, 1991   7/93

Book design by Patrice Fodero

Library of Congress Cataloging-in-Publication Data

De Mello, Anthony, 1931– 1987
  [Call to love]
  The way to love : the last meditations of Anthony de Mello /
Anthony de Mello.
      p.   cm.
  Originally published: Call to love. India : Gujarat Sahitya
Prakash, 1991.
  1. Meditations.   I. Title.
BX2182.2.D3868   1992
242—dc20   92-6243
                                                     CIP

ISBN 0-385-24938-1

CONTENTS

CONTENTS

INTRODUCTION

Years ago, when I first heard of Tony de Mello, S.J., I didn't believe what I heard. The story I am about to tell has bearing on the book you are about to read.

I was told that Tony gave a retreat to sixty fellow Jesuit priests and spoke to them six hours a day for eight days. I remember saying, "No Jesuit listens to another Jesuit six hours a day for eight days." When the fact was insisted on, I remember asking, "Who made that retreat?" The names of some very impressive Jesuits (impressive, at least, to me) were mentioned. It was then, like doubting Thomas in the Scriptures, I said, "This I have to see and hear for myself."

Thus began the journey with the man who would affect my life so profoundly that, years later, I wouldn't even recognize the person I was those years past. And not I alone, but thousands of others like me.

The occasion of my first meeting Tony de Mello now seems rather prosaic. He was asked to give a weekend retreat to a group of lay people. He agreed to do this on his way back to India from Rome. I asked to be put on that retreat just to meet and experience the man. It was an unforgettable weekend up in Saddle River, New Jersey, amid the snows of February.

I will never forget the feeling of liberation; the sense he made of spirituality, of prayer, of the meaning of life; his humor; his marvelous storytelling. And it was all done in such a personal style. Years later, when he was speaking by television satellite to more than three thousand college students, he maintained that personal style. "About twelve years ago," he remarked, "I discovered something that revolutionized my life." He had met a rickshaw driver in Calcutta named Rinsai, who, although he was dying of a painful disease and was so poor that he had to sell his skeleton before he died, still was a man filled with faith and interior joy. "I suddenly realized," Tony continued, "I was in the presence of a mystic who had rediscovered life. He was alive; I was dead. He was a man who had reincarnated himself during this life."

The reason I say that the story of my meeting Tony has bearing on the book you are about to read is because when I came upon this manuscript, although I was very familiar with all that he had written (and spoken), I was amazed at how these small but powerful "meditations" evoked in me the same feelings I experienced when I first encountered him. Just reading through these pages brought back the wonderful sense of challenge, the spiritual provocation that Tony was such a master at providing. There was a basic honesty in Tony de Mello's character with which he reevaluated everything in his own life. And it was this honesty that he communicated so effectively to all who would listen. His analogies, his stories, his telling criticism of sacred cows—all brilliantly peppered throughout this book—inspired in me a like reevaluation of my own life, and I have never regretted it.

Take each one of these meditations and carry it with you throughout your day. Challenge his ideas, mull over his thoughts, and then be silent. You will notice an effortless transformation taking place in your heart, the awakening experience of insight, the wonderful peace you experience when you gaze at the stars or watch a beautiful sunrise or glimpse a soft look of love in the eyes of your beloved. This is the effect these spiritual gems will have. All you need bring to them is a full heart and an inquiring mind.

J. Francis Stroud, S.J.
The Center for Spiritual Exchange
Fordham University
Bronx, N.Y.

THE WAY
TO LOVE

Profit and Loss

ॐ

For what will it profit a man, if he gains the whole world and forfeits his life?

—Matthew 16:26

Recall the kind of feeling you have when someone praises you, when you are approved, accepted, applauded. And contrast that with the kind of feeling that arises within you when you look at the sunset or the sunrise or Nature in general, or when you read a book or watch a movie that you thoroughly enjoy. Get the taste of this feeling and contrast it with the first, namely, the one that was generated within you when you were praised. Understand that the first type of feeling comes from self-glorification, self-promotion. It is a worldly feeling. The second comes from self-fulfillment, a soul feeling.

Here is another contrast: Recall the kind of

feeling you have when you succeed, when you have made it, when you get to the top, when you win a game or a bet or an argument. And contrast it with the kind of feeling you get when you really enjoy the job you are doing, you are absorbed in, the action that you are currently engaged in. And once again notice the qualitative difference between the worldly feeling and the soul feeling.

Yet another contrast: Remember what you felt like when you had power, you were the boss, people looked up to you, took orders from you; or when you were popular. And contrast that worldly feeling with the feeling of intimacy, companionship—the times you thoroughly enjoyed yourself in the company of a friend or with a group in which there was fun and laughter.

Having done this, attempt to understand the true nature of worldly feelings, namely, the feelings of self-promotion, self-glorification. They are not natural, they were invented by your society and your culture to make you productive and to make you controllable. These feelings do not produce the nourishment and happiness that is produced when one contemplates Nature or enjoys the company of one's friends or one's work. They were meant to produce thrills, excitement—and emptiness.

∾

Then observe yourself in the course of a day or a week and think how many actions of yours are performed, how many activities engaged in that are uncontaminated by the desire for these thrills, these excitements that only produce emptiness, the desire for attention, approval, fame, popularity, success or power.

And take a look at the people around you. Is there a single one of them who has not become addicted to these worldly feelings? A single one who is not controlled by them, hungers for them, spends every minute of his/her waking life consciously or unconsciously seeking them? When you see this you will understand how people attempt to gain the world and, in the process, lose their soul. For they live empty, soulless lives.

And here is a parable of life for you to ponder on: A group of tourists sits in a bus that is passing through gorgeously beautiful country; lakes and mountains and green fields and rivers. But the shades of the bus are pulled down. They do not have the slightest idea of what lies beyond the windows of the bus. And all the time of their journey is spent in squabbling over who will have the seat of honor in the bus, who will be applauded, who will be well considered. And so they remain till the journey's end.

DISCIPLESHIP

❧

IF ANYONE COMES TO ME AND DOES NOT HATE
HIS OWN FATHER AND MOTHER AND WIFE AND
CHILDREN AND BROTHERS AND SISTERS, YES,
AND EVEN HIS OWN LIFE, HE CANNOT BE MY
DISCIPLE.

—LUKE 14:26

Take a look at the world and see the unhappiness around you and in you. Do you know what
causes this unhappiness? You will probably say
loneliness or oppression or war or hatred or
atheism. And you will be wrong. There is only
one cause of unhappiness: the false beliefs you
have in your head, beliefs so widespread, so
commonly held, that it never occurs to you to
question them. Because of these false beliefs you
see the world and yourself in a distorted way.
Your programming is so strong and the pressure
of society so intense that you are literally

trapped into perceiving the world in this distorted kind of way. There is no way out, because you do not even have a suspicion that your perception is distorted, your thinking is wrong, and your beliefs are false.

Look around and see if you can find a single genuinely happy person—fearless, free from insecurities, anxieties, tensions, worries. You would be lucky if you found one in a hundred thousand. This should lead you to be suspicious of the programming and the beliefs that you and they hold in common. But you have also been programmed not to suspect, not to doubt, just to trust the assumptions that have been put into you by your tradition, your culture, your society, your religion. And if you are not happy, you have been trained to blame yourself, not your programming, not your cultural and inherited ideas and beliefs. What makes it even worse is the fact that most people are so brainwashed that they do not even realize how unhappy they are—like the man in a dream who has no idea he is dreaming.

What are these false beliefs that block you from happiness? Here are some examples. First: You cannot be happy without the things that you are attached to and that you consider so precious. False. There is not a single moment in your life when you do not have everything that you need to be happy. Think of that for a minute. The reason why you are unhappy is because you are focusing on what you do not have rather than on what you have right now.

Another belief: Happiness is in the future. Not true. Right here and now you are happy and you do not know it because your false beliefs and your distorted perceptions have got you caught up in fears, anxieties, attachments, conflicts, guilt and a host of games that you are programmed to play. If you would see through this you would realize that you are happy and do not know it.

Yet another belief: Happiness will come if you manage to change the situation you are in and the people around you. Not true. You stupidly squander so much energy trying to rearrange the world. If changing the world is your vocation in life, go right ahead and change it, but do not harbor the illusion that this is going to make you happy. What makes you happy or unhappy is not the world and the people around you, but the thinking in your head. As well search for an eagle's nest on the bed of an ocean, as search for happiness in the world outside of you. So if it is happiness that you seek you can stop wasting your energy trying to cure your baldness or build up an attractive body or change your residence or job or community or

lifestyle or even your personality. Do you realize
that you could change every one of these things,
you could have the finest looks and the most
charming personality and the most pleasant of
surroundings and still be unhappy? And deep
down you know this is true but still you waste
your effort and energy trying to get what you
know cannot make you happy.

Another false belief: If all your desires are
fulfilled you will be happy. Not true. In fact it is
these very desires and attachments that make
you tense, frustrated, nervous, insecure and
fearful. Make a list of all your attachments and
desires and to each of them say these words:
"Deep down in my heart I know that even after
I have got you I will not get happiness." And
ponder on the truth of those words. The fulfillment of desire can, at the most, bring flashes of
pleasure and excitement. Don't mistake that for
happiness.

What then is happiness? Very few people
know and no one can tell you, because happiness cannot be described. Can you describe light
to people who have been sitting in darkness all
their lives? Can you describe reality to someone
in a dream? Understand your darkness and it
will vanish; then you will know what light is.
Understand your nightmare for what it is and it
will stop; then you will wake up to reality. Un-

derstand your false beliefs and they will drop; then you will know the taste of happiness.

If people want happiness so badly, why don't they attempt to understand their false beliefs? First, because it never occurs to them to see them as false or even as beliefs. They see them as facts and reality, so deeply have they been programmed. Second, because they are scared to lose the only world they know: the world of desires, attachments, fears, social pressures, tensions, ambitions, worries, guilt, with flashes of the pleasure and relief and excitement which these things bring. Think of someone who is afraid to let go of a nightmare because, after all, that is the only world he knows. There you have a picture of yourself and of other people.

If you wish to attain to lasting happiness you must be ready to hate father, mother, even your own life and to take leave of all your possessions. How? Not by renouncing them or giving them up because what you give up violently you are forever bound to. But rather by seeing them for the nightmare they are; and then, whether you keep them or not, they will have lost their grip over you, their power to hurt you, and you will be out of your dream at last, out of your darkness, your fear, your unhappiness.

So spend some time seeing each of the things

you cling to for what it really is, a nightmare that causes you excitement and pleasure on the one hand but also worry, insecurity, tension, anxiety, fear, unhappiness on the other.

Father and mother: nightmare. Wife and children, brothers and sisters: nightmare. All your possessions: nightmare. Your life as it is now: nightmare. Every single thing you cling to and have convinced yourself you cannot be happy without: nightmare. Then you will hate father and mother, wife and children, brothers and sisters and even your own life. And you will so easily take leave of all your possessions, that is, you will stop clinging and thus have destroyed their capacity to hurt you. Then at last you will experience that mysterious state that cannot be described or uttered—the state of abiding happiness and peace. And you will understand how true it is that everyone who stops clinging to brothers or sisters, father, mother or children, land or houses . . . is repaid a hundred times over and gains eternal life.

THE EXTRA MILE

AND IF ANYONE WOULD SUE YOU AND TAKE
YOUR COAT, LET HIM HAVE YOUR CLOAK AS
WELL; AND IF ANYONE FORCES YOU TO GO ONE
MILE, GO WITH HIM TWO MILES.

—MATTHEW 5:40–41

If you take a look at the way you have been put
together and the way you function you will find
that inside your head there is a whole program,
a set of demands about how the world should
be, how you should be and what you should
want.

Who is responsible for the programming?
Not you. It isn't really you who decided even
such basics as your wants and desires and so-
called needs; your values, your tastes, your attitudes. It was your parents, your society, your
culture, your religion, your past experiences
who fed the operating instructions into your
computer. Now, however old you are or wherever you go, your computer goes along with you

and is active and operating at each conscious moment of the day, imperiously insisting that its demands be met by life, by people and by you. If the demands are met, the computer allows you to be peaceful and happy. If they are not met, even though it be through no fault of yours, the computer generates negative emotions that cause you to suffer.

For instance, when other people don't live up to your computer's expectations, it torments you with frustration or anger or bitterness. Another instance: When things are not under your control or the future is uncertain, your computer insists that you experience anxiety, tension, worry. Then you expend a lot of energy coping with these negative emotions. And you generally cope by expending more energy trying to rearrange the world around you so that the demands of your computer will be met. If that happens you will be granted a measure of precarious peace; precarious because at any moment some trifle (a delayed train, a tape recorder that doesn't work, a letter that doesn't arrive—anything) is going to be out of conformity with your computer's programming and the computer will insist that you become upset again.

And so you live a pathetic existence, constantly at the mercy of things and people, trying

❧

desperately to make them conform to your computer's demands, so that you can enjoy the only peace you can ever know—a temporary respite from negative emotions, courtesy of your computer and your programming.

Is there a way out? Yes. You are not going to be able to change your programming all that quickly, or perhaps ever. And you don't even need to. Try this: Imagine you are in a situation or with a person that you find unpleasant and that you would ordinarily avoid. Now observe how your computer instinctively becomes active, insisting that you avoid this situation or try to change it. And if you stay on there and refuse to change the situation, observe how the computer insists that you experience irritation or anxiety or guilt or some other negative emotion. Now keep looking at this unpleasant situation or person until you realize that it isn't they that are causing the negative emotions. They are just going their way, being themselves, doing their thing whether right or wrong, good or bad. It is your computer that, thanks to your programming, insists on your reacting with negative emotions. You will see this better if you realize that someone with a different programming when faced with this same situation or person or event would react quite calmly, even happily. Don't stop till you have grasped this truth: The only reason why you too are not reacting calmly and happily is your computer that is stubbornly insisting that reality be reshaped to conform to its programming. Observe all of this from the outside so to speak and see the marvelous change that comes about in you.

Once you have understood this truth and thereby stopped your computer from generating negative emotions you may take any action you deem fit. You may avoid the situation or the person; or you may try to change them; or you may insist on your rights or the rights of others being respected; you may even resort to the use of force. But only after you have got rid of your emotional upsets, for then your action will spring from peace and love, not from the neurotic desire to appease your computer or to conform to its programming or to get rid of the negative emotions it generates. Then you will understand how profound is the wisdom of the words: "If a man wants to sue you for your shirt, let him have your coat as well. If a man in authority makes you go one mile, go with him two." For it will have become evident to you that real oppression comes, not from people who fight you in court or from authority that subjects you to slave labor, but from your computer whose programming destroys your peace of mind the moment outside circumstances fail to conform to its demands. People have been known to be happy even in the oppressive atmosphere of a concentration camp! It is from the oppression of your programming that you need to be liberated. Only then will you experience that inner freedom from which alone all social revolution must arise for the powerful emotion, the passion that arises in your heart at the sight of social evils and impels you to action, will have its origin in reality, not in your programming or your ego.

HE WENT AWAY SAD

∽

AND THE YOUNG MAN WENT AWAY SORROW-
FUL, FOR HE HAD GREAT POSSESSIONS.

—MARK 10:22

Has it ever struck you that you have been programmed to be unhappy and so no matter what
you do to become happy, you are bound to fail?
It is as if you fed mathematical equations into a
computer and then failed each time you pushed
it to turn out lines from Shakespeare.

If you wish to be happy the first thing you
need is not effort or even goodwill or good
desires but a clear understanding of how exactly
you have been programmed. This is what happened: First your society and your culture
taught you to believe that you would not be
happy without certain persons and certain
things. Just take a look around you: Everywhere
people have actually built their lives on the un-

questioned belief that without certain things—money, power, success, approval, a good reputation, love, friendship, spirituality, God—they cannot be happy. What is your particular combination?

Once you swallowed your belief you naturally developed an attachment to this person or thing you were convinced you could not be happy without. Then came the efforts to acquire your precious thing or person, to cling to it once it was acquired, and to fight off every possibility of losing it. This finally led you to abject emotional dependence so that the object of your attachment had the power to *thrill* you when you attained it, to make you *anxious* lest you be deprived of it and *miserable* when you lost it. Stop for a moment now and contemplate in horror the endless list of attachments that you have become a prisoner to. Think of concrete things and persons, not abstractions . . . Once your attachment had you in its grip you began to strive might and main, every waking minute of your life, to rearrange the world around you so that you could attain and maintain the objects of your attachment. This is an exhausting task that leaves you little energy for the business of living and enjoying life fully. It is also an impossible task in an ever-changing world that you simply are not able to control. So instead of a life of serenity and fulfillment you are doomed to a life of frustration, anxiety, worry, insecurity, suspense, tension. For a few fleeting moments the world does, indeed, yield to your efforts and rearranges itself to suit your desires. Then you become briefly happy. Or rather, you experience a flash of pleasure which isn't happiness at all for it is accompanied by the underlying fear that at any moment this world of things and people that you have so painstakingly put in place will slip out of your control and let you down—which it never fails to do sooner or later.

And here is something else to ponder on: Each time you are anxious and afraid, it is because you may lose or fail to get the object of your attachment, isn't it? And each time you feel jealous, isn't it because someone may make off with what you are attached to? And almost all your anger comes from someone standing in the way of your attachment, doesn't it? And see how paranoid you become when your attachment is threatened—you cannot think objectively; your whole vision becomes distorted, doesn't it? And every time you feel bored, isn't it because you are not getting a sufficient supply of what you believe will make you happy, of what you are attached to? And when you are depressed and miserable, the cause is there for all to see: Life is not giving you what you have convinced yourself you cannot be happy without. Almost every negative emotion you experience is the direct outcome of an attachment.

So there you are loaded down by your attachments—and striving desperately to attain happiness precisely by holding on to the load. The very notion is absurd. The tragedy is that this is the only method that everyone has been taught for attaining happiness—a method guaranteed to produce anxiety, disappointment and sorrow. Hardly anyone has been told the following truth: In order to be genuinely happy there is one and only one thing you need to do: get deprogrammed, get rid of those attachments.

When people stumble upon this self-evident truth they become terrified at the thought of the pain involved in dropping their attachments. But the process is not a painful one at all. On the contrary, getting rid of attachments is a perfectly delightful task if the instrument you use to rid yourself of them is not willpower or renunciation but sight. All you need to do is open your eyes and see that you do not really need the object of your attachment at all; that you were programmed, brainwashed into thinking that you could not be happy or you could not live without this particular person or thing. Remember how heartbroken you once were, how you were certain you never would be happy again because you lost someone or something that was so precious to you? But then what happened? Time passed and you learned to get on pretty well, did you not? That should have alerted you to the falseness of your belief, to the trick your programmed mind was playing on you.

An attachment isn't a fact. It is a belief, a fantasy in your head, acquired through programming. If that fantasy did not exist inside your head, you would not be attached. You would love things and persons and you would enjoy them thoroughly but, lacking the belief, you would enjoy them on a nonattachment basis. As a matter of fact, is there any other way to really enjoy something? Pass in review now all those attachments of yours. And to each person or object that comes to mind say: "I am not really attached to you at all. I am merely deluding myself into the belief that without you I will not be happy." Just do this honestly and see the change that comes about within you: "I am not really attached to you at all. I have merely cheated myself into the belief that without you I will not be happy."

THE EYE OF A NEEDLE

༄

It is easier for a camel to go through the eye of a needle than for a rich man to enter the kingdom of God.

—MARK 10:25

What can one do to attain happiness? There is nothing you or anyone else can do. Why? For the simple reason that you are already happy right now. So how can you acquire what you already have? If that is so, why do you not experience this happiness which is already yours? Because your mind is creating unhappiness all the time. Drop this unhappiness of your mind and the happiness that has always been yours will instantly surface. How does one drop unhappiness? Find out what is causing it and look at the cause unflinchingly. It will automatically drop.

Now if you look carefully, you will see that there is one thing and only one thing that causes unhappiness. The name of that thing is Attachment. What is an attachment? An emotional state of clinging caused by the belief that without some particular thing or some person you cannot be happy. This emotional state of clinging is composed of two elements, one positive and the other negative. The positive element is the flash of pleasure and excitement, the thrill that you experience when you get what you are attached to. The negative element is the sense of threat and tension that always accompanies the attachment. Think of someone gobbling up food in a concentration camp; with one hand he brings the food to his mouth, with the other he protects it from neighbors who will grab it from him the moment he lowers his guard. There you have the perfect image of the attached person. So an attachment by its very nature makes you vulnerable to emotional turmoil and is always threatening to shatter your peace. So how can you expect an attached person to enter that ocean of happiness called the kingdom of God? As well expect a camel to pass through the eye of a needle!

Now the tragedy of an attachment is that if its object is not attained it causes unhappiness. But if it is attained, it does not cause happiness —it merely causes a flash of pleasure followed by weariness; and it is always accompanied, of course, by the anxiety that you may lose the object of your attachment. You will say, "Can't I keep just one attachment?" Of course. You can keep as many as you want. But for each attachment you pay a price in lost happiness. Think of this: The nature of attachments is such, that even if you satisfy many of them in the course of a single day, the one attachment that was not satisfied will prey upon your mind and make you unhappy. There is no way to win the battle of attachments. As well search for water without wetness as for an attachment without unhappiness. No one has ever lived who has come up with a formula for keeping the objects of one's attachments without struggle, anxiety, fear and, sooner or later, defeat.

There is only one way to win the battle of attachments: Drop them. Contrary to popular belief, dropping attachments is easy. All you have to do is see, but really *see,* the following truths. *First truth:* You are holding on to a false belief, namely, the belief that without this particular person or thing you will not be happy. Take your attachments one at a time and see the falseness of this belief. You may encounter resistance from your heart, but the moment you do see, there will be an immediate emotional result. At that very instant the attachment loses its force. *Second truth:* If you just enjoy things, refusing to let yourself be attached to them, that is, refusing to hold the false belief that you will not be happy without them, you are spared all the struggle and emotional strain of protecting them and guarding them for yourself. Has it occurred to you that you can keep all the objects of your attachments without giving them up, without renouncing a single one of them and you can enjoy them even more on a nonattachment, a nonclinging basis, because you are peaceful now and relaxed and unthreatened in your enjoyment of them? *The third and final truth:* If you learn to enjoy the scent of a thousand flowers you will not cling to one or suffer when you cannot get it. If you have a thousand favorite dishes, the loss of one will go unnoticed and leave your happiness unimpaired. But it is precisely your attachments that prevent you from developing a wider and more varied taste for things and people.

In the light of these three truths no attachment can survive. But the light must shine uninterruptedly if it is to be effective. Attachments can only thrive in the darkness of illusion. The rich man cannot enter the kingdom of joy not because he wants to be bad but because he chooses to be blind.

Nowhere to Go

&

FOXES HAVE HOLES, AND BIRDS OF THE AIR
HAVE NESTS; BUT THE SON OF MAN HAS NO-
WHERE TO LAY HIS HEAD.

—MATTHEW 8:20

Here is a mistake that most people make in their relationships with others. They try to build a steady nesting place in the ever-moving stream of life.

Think of someone whose love you desire. Do you want to be important to this person, to be especial and make a difference to his/her life? Do you want this person to care for you and be concerned about you in a special way? If you do, open your eyes and see that you are fool-ishly inviting others to reserve you for them-selves, to restrict your freedom for their benefit, to control your behavior, your growth and de-velopment so that it will suit their interest. It is as if the other person said to you, "If you want to be especial to me then you must meet my conditions. Because the moment you cease to live up to my expectations, you will cease to be especial." You wanted to be especial to someone, didn't you? So you must pay a price in lost freedom. You must dance to the other person's tune just as you demand that other persons dance to yours if they want to be especial to you.

Pause now to ask yourself if it is worth paying so much for so little. Imagine you say to this person whose special love you want, "Leave me free to be myself, to think my thoughts, to indulge my taste, to follow my inclination, to behave in ways that I decide are to my liking." The moment you say those words you will understand that you are asking for the impossible. To ask to be especial to someone means essentially to be bound to the task of making yourself pleasing to this person. And therefore to lose your freedom. Take all the time you need to realize this.

Maybe now you are ready to say, "I'd rather have my freedom than your love." If you could either have company in prison or walk the earth in freedom all alone, which would you choose? Now say to this person, "I leave you free to be yourself, to think your thoughts, to indulge your taste, follow your inclinations, behave in any way that you decide is to your liking." The moment you say that you will observe one of two things: Either your heart will resist those words and you will be exposed for the clinger and exploiter that you are; so now is the time to examine your false belief that without this person you cannot live or cannot be happy. Or your heart will pronounce the words sincerely and in that very instant all control, manipulation, exploitation, possessiveness, jealousy will drop. "I leave you free to be yourself: to think your thoughts, indulge your tastes, follow your inclinations, behave in ways that you decide are to your liking."

And you will notice something else: The person automatically ceases to be especial and important to you. And he/she becomes important the way a sunset or a symphony is lovely in itself, the way a tree is especial in itself and not for the fruit or the shade that it can offer you. Your beloved will then belong not to you but to everyone or to no one like the sunrise and the tree. Test it by saying those words again: "I leave you free to be yourself . . ." In saying those words you have set yourself free. You are now ready to love. For when you cling, what you offer the other is not love but a chain by which both you and your beloved are bound.

Love can only exist in freedom. The true lover seeks the good of his beloved which requires especially the liberation of the beloved from the lover.

Bring in the Poor

The householder in anger said to his servant, "Go out quickly to the streets and lanes of the city, and bring in the poor and maimed and blind and lame."

—Luke 14:21

Think of someone you dislike—someone you generally avoid because his/her presence generates negative feelings in you. Imagine yourself in this person's presence now and watch the negative emotions arise . . . you are, quite conceivably, in the presence of someone who is poor, crippled, blind or lame.

Now understand that if you invite this person, this beggar from the streets and alleys into your home, that is, into your presence, he/she will make you a gift that none of your charming, pleasant friends can make you, rich as they are. He or she is going to reveal yourself to you and reveal human nature to you—a revelation as precious as any found in Scripture, for what

∽

will it profit you to know all the Scriptures if you do not know yourself and so live the life of a robot? The revelation that this beggar is going to bring will widen your heart till there is room in it for every living creature. Can there be a finer gift than that?

Now take a look at yourself reacting negatively and ask yourself the following question: "Am I in charge of this situation or is this situation in charge of me?" That is the first revelation. With it comes the second: The way to be in charge of this situation is to be in charge of yourself, which you are not. How does one achieve this mastery? All you have to do is understand that there are people in the world who, if they were in your place, would not be negatively affected by this person. They would be in charge of the situation, above it, not subject to it as you are. Therefore, your negative feelings are caused, not by this person, as you mistakenly think, but by your programming. Here is the third and major revelation. See what happens when you really understand this.

Having received these revelations about yourself, listen to this revelation concerning human nature. This behavior, this trait in the other person that causes you to react negatively—do you realize that he or she is not responsible for it? You can hold on to your negative feelings only when you mistakenly believe that he or she is free and aware and therefore responsible. But who ever did evil in awareness? The ability to do evil or to be evil is not freedom but a sickness for it implies a lack of consciousness and sensitivity. Those who are truly free cannot sin as God cannot sin. This poor person here in front of you is crippled, blind, lame, not stubborn and malicious as you so foolishly thought. Understand this truth; look at it steadfastly and deeply; and you will see your negative emotions turn into gentleness and compassion. Suddenly you have room in your heart for someone who was consigned to the streets and alleys by others and by you.

Now you will realize that this beggar came to your home with an alms for you—the widening of your heart in compassion and the release of your spirit in freedom. Where before you used to be controlled (these persons had the power to create negative emotions in you and you went out of your way to avoid them) now you have the gift of freedom to avoid no one, to go anywhere. When you see this you will notice how to the feeling of compassion in your heart has been added the feeling of gratitude to this beggar who is your benefactor. And another new, unaccustomed feeling: You actually feel a desire to seek out the company of these growth-

producing crippled, blind and lame people, the
way someone who has learned to swim seeks
water, because each time you are with them,
where before you used to feel the oppression
and tyranny of negative feelings, you can now
actually feel an ever-expanding compassion and
the freedom of the skies. And you can barely
recognize yourself as you see yourself going out
into the streets and alleys of the town, in obedience to the Master's injunction, to bring in the
poor, the crippled, the blind and lame.

THE BLIND SEE

FOR JUDGMENT I CAME INTO THIS WORLD,
THAT THOSE WHO DO NOT SEE MAY SEE, AND
THAT THOSE WHO SEE MAY BECOME BLIND.

—JOHN 9:39

It is said that love is blind. But is it? Actually nothing on earth is as clear-sighted as love. The thing that is blind is not love but attachment. An attachment is a state of clinging that comes from the false belief that something or someone is necessary for your happiness. Do you have any attachments—people or things that you falsely believe you could not be happy without? Make a list of them right now before we go on to study how exactly they blind you.

Think of a politician who has convinced himself he will not be happy unless he gets political power. His quest for power coarsens his sensitivity to the rest of life. He barely has time for his family and friends. Suddenly all human beings are perceived and reacted to in terms of the support or threat that they are to his ambition. And those who can neither threaten nor support he does not even notice. If in addition to his craving for power he has an attachment to other things like sex or money, the poor man has become so selective in his perceptions that he could almost be said to be blind. Everyone sees this except the man himself. This is the condition that leads to the rejection of the Messiah, the rejection of truth and beauty and goodness, because one has come to be blind to perceive them.

Now think of yourself listening to an orchestra in which the sound of the drum is so loud that nothing else can be heard. To enjoy the symphony you must be responsive to every instrument in the orchestra. To be in the state called love you must be sensitive to the uniqueness and beauty of every single thing and person around you. You can hardly be said to love what you do not even notice; and if you notice only a few beings to the exclusion of others, that is not love at all, for love excludes no one at all; it embraces the whole of life; it listens to the symphony as a whole, not to just one or the other of the musical instruments.

Stop for a while now to see how your attachments drain life's symphony no less than the politician's attachment to power and the businessman's attachment to money have hardened them to the melody of life. Or look at the matter in another way: There is an enormous amount of information that is continuously flowing in from the world through the senses, the tissues of the organs of your body. Only a small part of this information reaches your conscious mind. It is like the infinite amount of feedback that is sent to the President of a nation: Only a tiny fraction finally makes its way to him. Somebody does the screening and the processing at the President's office. Who decides what will finally make its way to your conscious mind from all the material that is pouring in from the world? Three decisive filters: first your attachments, second your beliefs and third your fears.

Your attachments: You will inevitably look for what fosters or threatens them and turn a blind eye to the rest. You won't be interested in the rest anymore than the avaricious businessman is interested in anything that does not involve the making of money. Your beliefs: Just take a look at a fanatic who only notices what confirms his/her belief and blocks out whatever threatens it and you will understand what your beliefs are doing to you. And then your fears: If you knew you were to be executed in a week's time it would wonderfully concentrate your mind to the exclusion of everything else. That is what fears do; they irresistibly rivet your attention on to some things to the exclusion of others. You falsely think that your fears protect you, your beliefs have made you what you are and your attachments make your life exciting and secure. You fail to see that they are actually a screen between you and life's symphony.

It is quite impossible, of course, to be fully conscious of every note in life's symphony. But if your spirit becomes unclogged and your senses open you will begin to perceive things as they really are and to interact with reality and you will be entranced by the harmonies of the universe. Then you will understand what God is, for you will at last know what love is.

Look at it this way: You see persons and things not as they are but as you are. If you wish to see them as they are you must attend to your attachments and the fears that your attachments generate. Because when you look at life it is these attachments and fears that will decide what you will notice and what you block out. Whatever you notice then commands your attention. And since your looking has been selective you have an illusory version of the things and people around you. The more you live with this distorted version the more you become convinced that it is the only true picture of the world because your attachments and fears continue to process incoming data in a way that will reinforce your picture. This is what gives origin to your beliefs: fixed, unchanging ways of looking at a reality which is not fixed and unchanging at all but in movement and change. So it is no longer the real world that you interact with and love but a world created by your head. It is only when you drop your beliefs, your fears and the attachments that breed them that you will be freed from the insensitivity that makes you so deaf and blind to yourself and to the world.

Heaven at Hand

Repent, for the kingdom of heaven is at hand.

—Matthew 4:17

Imagine you have a radio that no matter how you turn the knob picks up only one station. You have no control over the volume. At times the sound is barely audible, at others, it is so loud that it almost shatters your eardrums. Moreover it is impossible to turn it off; at times it will be slow; it will suddenly begin to blare away when you want to rest and sleep. Who would put up with this kind of performance in a radio? And yet when your heart behaves in this kind of crazy fashion you not only put up with it but even call it normal and human.

Think of the numerous times you were tossed about by your emotions, that you have suffered the pangs of anger, depression, anxiety, when in every instance it was because your heart became set on getting something that you did not have, or on holding on to something that you had, or on avoiding something that you did not want. You were in love and you felt rejected or jealous; suddenly all your mind and heart became focused on this one thing, and the banquet of life turned to ashes in your mouth. You were bent on winning an election and in the din of battle it was impossible to hear the songs of birds: Your ambition drowned out every other sound. You were faced with the possibility of a serious illness or the loss of a loved one and you found it impossible to concentrate on anything.

To put it briefly, the moment you pick up an attachment, the functioning of this lovely apparatus called the human heart is destroyed. If you want to repair your radio, you must study radio mechanics. If you want to reform your heart, you must give serious, prolonged thought to four liberating truths. But first choose some attachment that troubles you, something that you are clinging to, or something that you dread, or something you are craving for, and keep this attachment in mind as you listen to these truths.

The first truth: You must choose between your attachment and happiness. You cannot have both. The moment you pick up an attachment, your heart is thrown out of kilter and your ability to lead a joyful carefree serene life is destroyed. See how true this is when applied to the attachment that you have chosen.

The second truth: Where did your attachment come from? You were not born with it. It sprang from a lie that your society and your culture have told you, or a lie that you have told yourself, namely, that without this or the other, without this person or the other, you can't be happy. Just open your eyes and see how false this is. There are hundreds of persons who are perfectly happy without this thing or person or situation that you crave for and that you have convinced yourself you cannot live without. So make your choice: Do you want your attachment, or your freedom and happiness?

The third truth: If you wish to be fully alive you must develop a sense of perspective. Life is infinitely greater than this trifle your heart is attached to and which you have given the power to so upset you. Trifle, yes, because if you live long enough a day will easily come when it will cease to matter. It will not even be remembered —your own experience will confirm this. Just as today you barely remember, are no longer the least bit affected by those tremendous trifles that so disturbed you in the past.

And so the fourth truth brings you to the

unavoidable conclusion that no thing or person outside of you has the power to make you happy or unhappy. Whether you are aware of it or not it is you and only you who decides to be happy or unhappy, whether you will cling to your attachment or not in any given situation.

As you ponder these truths you may become aware that your heart is resisting them or argues against them and refuses to look at them. That is a sign that you have not yet suffered enough at the hand of your attachments to really want to do something about your spiritual radio. Or your heart may place no resistance to these truths; if that is so, rejoice. Repentance, the re-fashioning of the heart has begun and the kingdom of God—the gratefully carefree life of children—has come within your grasp at last and you are about to reach out and take possession of it.

What Must I Do?

❧

"TEACHER, WHAT GOOD DEED MUST I DO, TO
HAVE ETERNAL LIFE?"

—MATTHEW 19:16

Think of yourself in a concert hall listening to
the strains of the sweetest music when you suddenly remember that you forgot to lock your
car. You are anxious about the car, you cannot
walk out of the hall and you cannot enjoy the
music. There you have a perfect image of life as
it is lived by most human beings.

For life to those who have the ears to hear is
a symphony; but very, very rare indeed is the
human being who hears the music. Why? Because they are busy listening to the noises that
their conditioning and their programming have
put into their heads. That and something else—
their attachments. An attachment is a major
killer of life. To really hear the symphony you

must be sensitively attuned to every instrument in the orchestra. When you take pleasure only in the drum, you cease to hear the symphony because the sound of the drum has blotted out the other instruments. You may have your preferences for drum or violin or piano; no harm in these, for a preference does not damage your capacity to hear and enjoy the other instruments. But the moment your preference turns into an attachment, it hardens you to the other sounds, you suddenly undervalue them. And it blinds you to its particular instrument, for you give it a value out of all proportion to its merit.

Now look at a person or a thing you have an attachment for: someone or something to whom you have handed over the power to make you happy or unhappy. Observe how, because of your concentration on getting this person or thing and holding on to it and enjoying it exclusively to the exclusion of other things and persons; and how, because of your obsession with this person or thing, you have less sensitivity to the rest of the world. You have become hardened. And have the courage to see how prejudiced and blind you have become in the presence of this object of your attachment.

When you see this you will feel a yearning to rid yourself of every attachment. The problem is, how? Renunciation and avoidance is no help, for to blot out the sound of the drum once again makes you as hard and insensitive as to concentrate solely on the drum. What you need is not renunciation but understanding, awareness. If your attachments have caused you suffering and sorrow, that's a help to understanding. If you have at least once in your life had the sweet taste of freedom and the delight in life that unattachment brings, that too is a help. It also helps to consciously notice the sound of the other instruments in the orchestra. But there is no substitute for the awareness that shows you the loss you suffer when you overvalue the drum and when you turn a deaf ear to the rest of the orchestra.

The day that happens and your attachment to the drum drops, you will no longer say to your friend, "How happy you have made me." For in so saying you flatter his ego and manipulate him into wanting to please you again. And you give yourself the illusion that your happiness depends on your friend. Rather you will say, "When you and I met, happiness arose." That leaves the happiness uncontaminated by his ego and yours. Neither of you can take the credit for it. And that makes it possible for the two of you to part with no attachment to each other, or to the experience which your meeting generated, for you have enjoyed, not each other, but the symphony that arose in your meeting. And when you move on to the next situation, or person, or work, you do so without any emotional carryover. And then you make the joyful discovery that the symphony arises there too, playing a different melody in the next situation, and the next, and the next.

Now you will move through life living from one moment to the other, wholly absorbed in the present, carrying with you so little from the past that your spirit could pass through the eye of a needle; as little distracted by the worries of the future as the birds of the air and the flowers of the field. You will be attached to no person or thing, for you will have developed a taste for the symphony of life. And you will love life alone with the passionate attachment of your whole heart and your whole soul and your whole mind and all your strength. You will find yourself traveling unencumbered and free as a bird in the sky, always living in the Eternal Now. And you will have found in your heart the answer to the question, "Master, what is it that I must do to get eternal life?"

No Stone Will Be Left

Think of a flabby person covered with layers of fat. That is what your mind can become—flabby, covered with layers of fat till it becomes too dull and lazy to think, to observe, to explore, to discover. It loses its alertness, its aliveness, its flexibility and goes to sleep. Look around you and you will see almost everyone with minds like that: dull, asleep, protected by layers of fat, not wanting to be disturbed or questioned into wakefulness.

What are these layers? Every belief that you hold, every conclusion you have reached about

45

persons and things, every habit and every attachment. In your formative years you should
have been helped to scrape off these layers and
liberate your mind. Instead your society, your
culture, which put these layers on your mind in
the first place, has educated you to not even notice them, to go to sleep and let other people—
the experts: your politicians, your cultural and
religious leaders—do your thinking for you. So
you are weighed down with the load of unex-
amined, unquestioned authority and tradition.

Let us examine these layers one at a time.
First your beliefs. If you experience life as a
communist or a capitalist, as a Moslem or a
Jew, you are experiencing life in a prejudiced,
slanted way; there is a barrier, a layer of fat
between Reality and you because you no longer
see and touch it directly.

Second layer: your ideas. If you hold on to
an idea about someone, then you no longer love
that person but your idea of that person. You
see him/her do or say something or behave in a
certain kind of way and you slap a label on: She
is silly or he is dull or he is cruel or she is very
sweet, etc. So now you have a screen, a layer of
fat between you and this person because when
you next meet him/her you will experience them
in terms of that idea of yours even though they

4 6

have changed. Observe how you have done this with almost everyone you know.

Third layer: habits. A habit is essential to human living. How would we ever walk or speak or drive a car unless we relied on habit? But habits must be limited to things mechanical —not to love or to sight. Who wants to be loved from habit? Have you ever sat on a seashore spellbound by the majesty and the mystery of the ocean? A fisherman looks at the ocean daily and does not notice its grandeur. Why? The dulling effect of a layer of fat called habit. You have formed fixed ideas of all the things you see and, when encountering them, it is not them you see in all their changing freshness, but the same dull, thick, boring idea acquired through habit. And that is how you deal with people and with things, how you relate to them: no freshness, no newness, but the same dull, routine (boring) ways produced by habit. You are incapable of looking in other, more creative ways, for, having developed a habit for dealing with the world and with people, you can put your mind on automatic pilot and go to sleep.

Fourth layer: your attachments and your fears. This layer is the easiest to see. Put a thick coating of attachment, of fear (and therefore dislike) on to anything or anyone—in that very instant you cease to see that person or thing as it really is. Just recall some of the persons you dislike or fear or are attached to and you will see how true this is.

Do you see now how you are in a prison created by the beliefs and traditions of your society and culture and by the ideas, prejudices, attachments and fears of your past experiences? Wall upon wall surrounds your prison cell so that it seems almost impossible that you will ever break out and make contact with the richness of life and love and freedom that lies beyond your prison fortress. And yet the task, far from being impossible, is actually easy and delightful. What can you do to break out? Four things: First, realize that you are surrounded by prison walls, that your mind has gone to sleep. It does not even occur to most people to see this, so they live and die as prison inmates. Most people end up being conformists; they adapt to prison life. A few become reformers; they fight for better living conditions in the prison, better lighting, better ventilation. Hardly anyone becomes a rebel, a revolutionary who breaks down the prison walls. You can only be a revolutionary when you see the prison walls in the first place.

Second, contemplate the walls, spend hours just observing your ideas, your habits, your attachments and your fears without any judgment and condemnation. Look at them and they will crumble.

Third, spend some time observing the things and people around you. Look, but really look, as if for the very first time, at the face of a friend, a leaf, a tree, a bird in flight, the behavior and mannerisms of the people around you. Really see them and hopefully you will see them afresh as they are in themselves without the dulling, stupefying effect of your ideas and habits.

The fourth and most important step: Sit down quietly and observe how your mind functions. There is a steady flow of thoughts and feelings and reactions there. Watch the whole of it for long stretches of time the way you watch a river or a movie. You will soon find it so much more absorbing than any river or movie. And so much more life-giving and liberating. After all can you even be said to be alive if you are not even conscious of your own thoughts and reactions? The unaware life, it is said, is not worth living. It cannot even be called life; it is a mechanical, robot existence; a sleep, an unconsciousness, a death; and yet this is what people call human life!

So watch, observe, question, explore and your mind will come alive and shed its fat and become keen and alert and active. Your prison walls will come tumbling down till not one stone of the Temple will be left upon another, and you will be blessed with the unimpeded vision of things as they are, the direct experience of Reality.

How to Give?

❧

WHEN YOU GIVE ALMS, DO NOT LET YOUR
LEFT HAND KNOW WHAT YOUR RIGHT HAND IS
DOING.

—MATTHEW 6:3

It is with charity as with happiness and holiness.
It is not possible for you to say that you are
happy because the moment you become conscious of your happiness you cease to be happy.
What you call the experience of happiness is not
happiness at all but the excitement and thrill
caused by some person or thing or event. True
happiness is uncaused. You are happy for no
reason at all. And true happiness cannot be experienced. It is not within the realm of consciousness. It is unself-consciousness.

So it is with holiness. The moment you are
aware of your holiness it goes sour and becomes
self-righteousness. A good deed is never so good
as when you have no consciousness that it is

good—you are so much in love with the action that you are quite unselfconscious about your goodness and virtue. Your left hand has no idea that your right hand is doing something good or meritorious. You simply do it because it seems the natural, spontaneous thing to do. Spend some time in becoming aware of the fact that all the virtue that you can see in yourself is no virtue at all but something that you have cunningly cultivated and produced and forced on yourself. If it were real virtue you would have enjoyed it thoroughly and would feel so natural that it wouldn't occur to you to think of it as a virtue. So the first quality of holiness is its unself-consciousness.

The second quality is its effortlessness. Effort can change behavior, it cannot change you. Think of this: Effort can put food into your mouth, it cannot produce an appetite; it can keep you in bed, it cannot produce sleep; it can make you reveal a secret to another but it cannot produce trust; it can force you to pay a compliment, it cannot produce genuine admiration; effort can perform acts of service, it is powerless to produce love or holiness. All you can achieve by your effort is repression, not genuine change and growth. Change is only brought about by awareness and understanding. Understand your unhappiness and it will disappear—what results is the state of happiness. Understand your pride and it will drop—what results will be humility. Understand your fears and they will melt—the resultant state is love. Understand your attachments and they will vanish—the consequence is freedom. Love and freedom and happiness are not things that you can cultivate and produce. You cannot even know what they are. All you can do is observe their opposites and, through your observation, cause these opposites to die.

There is a third quality of holiness: It cannot be desired. If you desire happiness you will be anxious lest you do not attain it. You will be constantly in a state of dissatisfaction; and dissatisfaction and anxiety kill the very happiness that they set out to gain. When you desire holiness for yourself you feed the very greed and ambition that make you so selfish and vain and unholy.

Here is something you must understand: There are two sources for change within you. One is the cunningness of your ego that pushes you into making efforts to become something other than you are meant to be so that it can give itself a boost, so that it can glorify itself. The other is the wisdom of Nature. Thanks to this wisdom you become aware, you understand it. That is all you do, leaving the change—type, the manner, the speed, the time of change—to

Reality and to Nature. Your ego is a great technician. It cannot be creative. It goes in for methods and techniques and produces so-called holy people who are rigid, consistent, mechanical, lifeless, as intolerant of others as they are of themselves—violent people the very opposite of holiness and love. The type of "spiritual" people who, conscious of their spirituality, then proceed to crucify the Messiah. Nature is not a technician. Nature is creative. You will be a creator, not a wily technician when there is abandonment in you—no greed, no ambition, no anxiety, no sense of striving, gaining, arriving, attaining. All there is, is a keen, alert, penetrating, vigilant awareness that causes the dissolution of all one's foolishness and selfishness, all one's attachments and fears. The changes that follow are not the result of your blueprints and efforts but the product of Nature that spurns your plans and will, thereby leaving no room for a sense of merit or achievement or even any consciousness on the part of your left hand of what Reality is doing by means of your right.

SERPENTS AND DOVES

So be wise as serpents and innocent as doves.

—MATTHEW 10:16

Observe the wisdom that operates in doves and in flowers and trees and the whole of Nature. It is the same wisdom that does for us what our brain could never do: It circulates our blood, digests our food, pumps our hearts, expands our lungs, immunizes our bodies and heals our wounds while our conscious minds are engaged in other matters. This kind of Nature-wisdom we are only now beginning to discover in so-called primitive peoples who, like the dove, are so simple and wise.

We who consider ourselves more advanced have developed another kind of wisdom, the cunningness of the brain, for we have realized that we can improve on Nature and provide ourselves with safety and protection and length of life and speed and comfort unknown to primitive peoples. All of this thanks to a fully developed brain. Our challenge is to recapture the simplicity and wisdom of the dove without losing the cunningness of the serpentine brain.

How can you achieve this? Through an important realization, namely, that every time you strive to improve on Nature by going against it, you will damage yourself, for Nature is your very being. It is as if your right hand were to fight your left hand or your right foot were to stamp on your left foot. Both sides lose and, instead of being creative and alive, you are locked in conflict. This is the state of most people in the world. Take a look at them: dead, uncreative, stuck because they are locked in conflict with Nature, attempting to improve themselves by going against what their nature demands. In a conflict between Nature and your brain, back Nature; if you fight her, she will eventually destroy you. The secret therefore is to improve on Nature in harmony with Nature. How can you achieve this harmony?

First: Think of some change that you wish to bring about in your life or in your personality. Are you attempting to force this change on your nature through effort and through the desire to become something that your ego has planned?

That is the serpent fighting the dove. Or are you content to study, observe, understand, be aware of your present state and problems, without pushing, without forcing things that your ego desires, leaving Reality to effect changes according to Nature's plans, not yours? Then you have the perfect blending of the serpent and the dove. Take a look at some of those problems of yours, those changes you desire in yourself, and observe your way of going about it. See how you attempt to bring about change—both in yourself and in others—through the use of punishment and reward, through discipline and control, through sermonizing and guilt, through greed and pride, ambition and vanity, rather than through loving acceptance and patience, painstaking understanding and vigilant awareness.

Second: Think of your body and compare it with the body of an animal that is left in its natural habitat. The animal is never overweight, never tense except before fight or flight. It never eats or drinks what is not good for it. It has all the rest and exercise that it needs. It has the right amount of exposure to the elements, to wind and sun and rain and heat and cold. That is because the animal listens to its body and allows itself to be guided by the body's wisdom. Compare that with your own foolish cunningness. If your body could speak, what would it say to you? Observe the greed, the ambition, the vanity, the desire to show off and to please others, the guilt that drives you to ignore the voice of your body while you chase after objectives set by your ego. You have indeed lost the simplicity of the dove.

Third: Ask yourself how much you are in touch with Nature, with trees and earth and grass and sky and wind and rain and sun and flowers and birds and animals. How much are you exposed to Nature? How much do you commune with her, observe her, contemplate her in wonder, identify with her? When your body is too long withdrawn from the elements, it withers, it becomes flabby and fragile because it has been isolated from its life force. When you are too long separated from Nature, your spirit withers and dies because it has been wrenched from its roots.

MEN OF VIOLENCE

ℰ

THE KINGDOM OF HEAVEN HAS SUFFERED VIO-
LENCE, AND MEN OF VIOLENCE TAKE IT BY
FORCE.

—MATTHEW 11:12

Compare the serene and simple splendor of a
rose in bloom with the tensions and restlessness
of your life. The rose has a gift that you lack: It
is perfectly content to be itself. It has not been
programmed from birth, as you have been, to be
dissatisfied with itself, so it has not the slightest
urge to be anything other than it is. That is why
it possesses the artless grace and absence of inner conflict that among humans is only found in
little children and mystics.

Consider your sad condition. You are always dissatisfied with yourself, always wanting
to change yourself. So you are full of violence
and self-intolerance which only grows with every effort that you make to change yourself. So

any change you achieve is always accompanied by inner conflict. And you suffer when you see others achieve what you have not and become what you are not.

Would you be tormented by jealousy and envy if, like the rose, you were content to be what you are and never aspired to what you are not? But you are driven, are you not, to be like someone else who has more knowledge, better looks, more popularity or success than you. You want to become more virtuous, more loving, more meditative; you want to find God, to come closer to your ideals. Think of the sad history of your efforts at self-improvement, that either ended in disaster or succeeded only at the cost of struggle and pain. Now suppose you desisted from all efforts to change yourself, and from all self-dissatisfaction, would you then be doomed to go to sleep having passively accepted everything in you and around you? There is another way besides laborious self-pushing on the one hand and stagnant acceptance on the other. It is the way of self-understanding. This is far from easy because to understand what you are requires complete freedom from all desire to change what you are into something else. You will see this if you compare the attitude of a scientist who studies the habits of ants without the slightest desire to change them with the attitude of a dog trainer who studies the habits of a dog with a view to making it learn something. If what you attempt is not to change yourself but to observe yourself, to study every one of your reactions to people and things, without judgment or condemnation or desire to reform yourself, your observation will be nonselective, comprehensive, never fixed on rigid conclusions, always open and fresh from moment to moment. Then you will notice a marvelous thing happening within you: You will be flooded with the light of awareness, you will become transparent and transformed.

Will change occur then? Oh, yes. In you and in your surroundings. But it will not be brought about by your cunning, restless ego that is forever competing, comparing, coercing, sermonizing, manipulating in its intolerance and its ambitions, thereby creating tension and conflict and resistance between you and Nature—an exhausting, self-defeating process like driving with your brakes on. No, the transforming light of awareness brushes aside your scheming, self-seeking ego to give Nature full rein to bring about the kind of change that she produces in the rose: artless, graceful, unself-conscious, wholesome, untainted by inner conflict.

Since all change is violent she will be violent. But the marvelous quality of Nature-violence, unlike ego-violence, is that it does not spring from intolerance and self-hatred. So there is no anger in the rainstorm that carries everything before it, or the fish that devour their young in obedience to ecological laws we know not, or body cells when they destroy each other in the interest of a higher good. When Nature destroys, it is not from ambition or greed or self-aggrandizement, but in obedience to mysterious laws that seek the good of the whole universe above the survival and well-being of the parts.

It is this kind of violence that arises within mystics who storm against ideas and structures that have become entrenched in their societies and cultures when awareness awakens them to evils their contemporaries are blind to. It is this violence that causes the rose to come into being in the face of forces hostile to it. And it is to this violence that the rose, like the mystic, will sweetly succumb after it has opened its petals to the sun and lives in fragile, feeling loveliness, quite unconcerned to add a single extra minute to its allotted span of life. And so it lives in blessedness and beauty like the birds of the air and the flowers of the field, with no trace of the restlessness and dissatisfaction, the jealousy and anxiety and competitiveness that characterize the world of human beings who seek to control and coerce rather than be content to flower into awareness, leaving all change to the mighty force of God in Nature.

Show No Partiality

∽

"TEACHER," THEY SAID, "WE KNOW THAT YOU
SPEAK AND TEACH RIGHTLY, AND SHOW NO
PARTIALITY."

—LUKE 20:21

Look at your life and see how you have filled its
emptiness with people. As a result they have a
stranglehold on you. See how they control your
behavior by their approval and disapproval.
They hold the power to ease your loneliness
with their company, to send your spirits soaring
with their praise, to bring you down to the
depths with their criticism and rejection. Take a
look at yourself spending almost every waking
minute of your day placating and pleasing people, whether they are living or dead. You live by
their norms, conform to their standards, seek
their company, desire their love, dread their rid-
icule, long for their applause, meekly submit to
the guilt they lay upon you; you are terrified to

go against the fashion in the way you dress or speak or act or even think.

And observe how even when you control them you depend on them and are enslaved by them.

People have become so much a part of your being that you cannot even imagine living a life that is unaffected or uncontrolled by them. As a matter of fact, they have convinced you that if you ever broke free of them, you would become an island—solitary, bleak, unloving. But the exact opposite is true. How can you love someone whom you are a slave to? How can you love someone whom you cannot live without? You can only desire, need, depend and fear and be controlled. Love is to be found only in fearlessness and freedom. How do you achieve this freedom? By means of a two-pronged attack on your dependency and slavery. First, awareness. It is next to impossible to be dependent, to be a slave, when one constantly observes the folly of one's dependence. But awareness may not be enough for a person whose addiction is people. You must cultivate activities that you love. You must discover work that you do, not for its utility, but for itself. Think of something that you love to do for itself, whether it succeeds or not, whether you are praised for it or not, whether you are loved and rewarded for it or not, whether people know about it and are grateful to you for it or not. How many activities can you count in your life that you engage in simply because they delight you and grip your soul? Find them out, cultivate them, for they are your passport to freedom and to love.

Here too you have probably been brainwashed into the following consumeristic way of thinking: To enjoy a poem or a landscape or a piece of music seems a waste of time; you must produce a poem or a composition or a work of art. Even to produce it is of little value in itself; your work must be known. What good is it if no one ever knows it? And even if it is known, that means nothing if it is not applauded and praised by people. Your work achieves maximum value if it becomes popular and sells! So you are back again into the arms and control of people. The value of an action, according to them, is not in its being loved and done and enjoyed for itself, but in its success.

The royal road to mysticism and to Reality does not pass through the world of people. It passes through the world of actions that are engaged in for themselves without an eye to success or to gain—or profit actions. Contrary to popular beliefs, the cure for lovelessness and loneliness is not company but contact with Reality. The moment you touch this Reality you will know what freedom and love are. Freedom from people—and so the ability to love them.

You must not think for love to arise in your heart, you must first meet people. That would not be love but attraction or compassion. Rather it is love that first springs in the heart through your contact with the Real. Not love for any particular person or thing but the reality of love—an attitude, a disposition of love. This love then radiates outward to the world of things and persons.

If you desire this love to exist in your life you must break loose from your inward dependence on people by becoming aware of it and by engaging in activities that you love to do for themselves.

ONE TEACHER

BUT YOU ARE NOT TO BE CALLED RABBI, FOR
YOU HAVE ONE TEACHER, AND YOU ARE ALL
BRETHREN.

—MATTHEW 20:8

You can get someone to teach you things mechanical or scientific or mathematical like algebra or English or riding a cycle or operating a computer. But in the things that really matter, life, love, reality, God, no one can teach you a thing. All they can do is give you formulas. And as soon as you have a formula, you have reality filtered through the mind of someone else. If you take those formulas you will be imprisoned. You will wither and when you come to die you will not have known what it means to see for yourself, to learn.

Look at it this way: There have been moments in your life when you had an experience that you know you will have to carry with you to your grave because you are quite unable to find words with which to communicate the experience to anyone. As a matter of fact there simply are no words in any human language to communicate exactly what you experienced. Think of the kind of feeling that came upon you when you saw a bird fly over a lake or observed a blade of grass peeping out of a crack in the wall or heard the cry of a baby at night or sensed the loveliness of a naked human body or gazed at a corpse lying cold and rigid in a coffin. You may try to communicate the experience in music or poetry or painting. But in your heart you know that no one will ever comprehend exactly what it was you saw and sensed. This is something you are quite powerless to express, much less teach, to another human being.

That is exactly how a Master feels when you ask him to teach you about life or God or reality. All he can do is give you a formula, a set of words strung together into a formula. But of what use are those words? Imagine a group of tourists in a bus. The shades of the bus are down and they don't see or hear or touch or smell a single thing from the strange exotic country that they are passing through, while all the while their guide chatters away, giving them what he thinks is a vivid description of the smells, sounds and sights of the world outside.

The only things they will experience are the images that his words create in their heads. And let's suppose the bus stops and he sends them forth with formulas about what they can expect to see and experience. Their experience will be contaminated, conditioned, distorted by those formulas and they will perceive, not the Reality itself but Reality as filtered through the guide's formulas.

They will look at Reality selectively or they will project their own formulas onto it, so it is not Reality they will see but a confirmation of their formulas.

Is there any way you can know that what you are in touch with is Reality? Here is one sign: What you perceive does not fit into any formula whether given by another or created by yourself. It simply cannot be put into words. So what can teachers do? They can bring to your notice what is unreal, they cannot show you Reality; they can destroy your formulas, they cannot make you see what the formula is pointing to; they can indicate your error, they cannot put you in possession of the Truth. They can, at the most, point in the direction of Reality, they cannot tell you what to see. You will have to walk out there all alone and discover for yourself.

To walk alone—that means to walk away from every formula—the ones given to you by others, the ones you learned from books, the ones that you yourself invented in the light of your own past experience. That is possibly the most terrifying thing a human being can do: move into the unknown, unprotected by any formula. To walk away from the world of human beings as the prophets and the mystics did is not to walk away from their company but from their formulas. Then, even though you are surrounded by people, you are truly and utterly alone. What an awesome solitude! That solitude, that aloneness is Silence. It is only this Silence that you will see. And the moment you see you will abandon every book and guide and guru.

What is it that you will see? Anything, everything: a falling leaf, the behavior of a friend, the ripples on the surface of a lake, a pile of stones, a ruined building, a crowded street, a starry sky, whatever. After you have seen, someone may attempt to help you put your vision into words but you will shake your head No, not that— that's just another formula. Someone else will attempt to explain the meaning of what you saw and you will shake your head again because meaning is a formula, something that can be put into concepts and makes sense to the thinking mind, and what you saw is beyond all formula, all meaning. And a strange change will come about in you, barely perceptible at first but radically transforming. Because, having seen, you will never be the same again. You will feel the exhilarating freedom, the extraordinary confidence that comes from knowing that every formula, no matter how sacred, is worthless; and you will never again call anyone your teacher. Then you will never cease to learn as each day you observe and understand afresh the whole process and movement of life. Then every single thing will be your teacher.

So put your books and formulas aside; dare to abandon your teacher whoever your teacher may be and see things for yourself. Dare to look at everything around you without fear and without formula and it won't be long before you see.

BECOME LIKE CHILDREN

∽

TRULY, I SAY TO YOU, UNLESS YOU TURN AND
BECOME LIKE CHILDREN, YOU WILL NEVER
ENTER THE KINGDOM OF HEAVEN.

—MATTHEW 18:3

The first quality that strikes one when one looks
into the eyes of a child is its innocence: its lovely
inability to lie or wear a mask or pretend to be
anything other than what it is. In this the child
is exactly like the rest of Nature. A dog is a dog;
a rose, a rose; a star, a star; everything is quite
simply what it is. Only the adult human being is
able to be one thing and pretend to be another.
When grown-ups punish a child for telling the
truth, for revealing what it thinks and feels, the
child learns to dissemble and its innocence is
destroyed. Soon it will join the ranks of the
numberless people who say helplessly, "I do not
know who I am," for, having hidden the truth

about themselves for so long from others, they end up by hiding it from themselves. How much of the innocence of childhood do you still retain, is there anyone today in whose presence you can be simply and totally yourself, as nakedly open and innocent as a child?

There is another more subtle way in which the innocence of childhood is lost: when the child is infected by the desire to become somebody. Contemplate the crowds of people who are striving might and main to become, not what Nature intended them to be—musicians, cooks, mechanics, carpenters, gardeners, inventors—but somebody: to become successful, famous, powerful; to become something that will bring, not quiet self-fulfillment, but self-glorification, self-expansion. You are looking at people who have lost their innocence because they have chosen not to be themselves but to promote themselves, to show off, even if it be only in their own eyes. Look at your daily life. Is there a single thought, word or action untainted by the desire to become somebody, even if all you seek to become is a spiritual success or a saint unknown to anyone except yourself? The child, like the innocent animal, surrenders to its nature to be and become quite simply what it is. Adults who have preserved their innocence also surrender like the child to the impulse of Nature or Destiny without a thought to become somebody or to impress others; but, unlike the child, they rely, not on instinct, but on ceaseless awareness of everything in them and around them; that awareness shields them from evil and brings about the growth that was intended for them by Nature, not designed by their ambitious egos.

Here is another way that grown-ups corrupt the innocence of childhood: They teach the child to imitate someone. The moment you make the child a carbon copy you stamp out the spark of originality with which it came into the world. The moment you choose to become like someone else however great or holy, you have prostituted your being. Think sadly of the divine spark of uniqueness that lies within you, buried under layers of fear. The fear that you will be ridiculed or rejected if you dare to be yourself and refuse to conform mechanically in the way you dress and act and think. See how you conform not only in your actions and thoughts but even in your reactions, your emotions, your attitudes, your values. You dare not break out of this prostitution and reclaim your original innocence. This is the price you pay for the passport of acceptance by your society or organization. So you enter the world of the crooked and the controlled and are exiled from

∽

the kingdom that belongs to the innocence of childhood.

One final subtle way you destroy your innocence is when you compete and compare yourself with others. When you do that you exchange your simplicity for the ambition of wanting to be as good as someone else or even better. Think of this: The reason why the child is able to preserve its innocence and live like the rest of creation in the bliss of the kingdom is that it has not been sucked into what we call the world—that region of darkness inhabited by grown-ups whose lives are spent not in living but in courting applause and admiration; not in blissfully being themselves but in neurotically comparing and competing, striving for those empty things called success and fame even if they can be attained only at the expense of defeating, humiliating, destroying their neighbors. If you allow yourself to really feel the pains of this hell on earth, the utter emptiness it brings, you might experience within you a revolt, a disgust so powerful that it will shatter the chains of dependence and deceit that have been forged around your soul and you will break loose into the kingdom of innocence where mystics and children dwell.

LOVE ONE ANOTHER

THIS IS MY COMMANDMENT, THAT YOU LOVE
ONE ANOTHER AS I HAVE LOVED YOU.

—JOHN 15:12

What is love? Take a look at a rose. Is it possible
for the rose to say, "I shall offer my fragrance to
good people and withhold it from bad people?"
Or can you imagine a lamp that withholds its
rays from a wicked person who seeks to walk in
its light? It could only do that by ceasing to be a
lamp. And observe how helplessly and indis-
criminately a tree gives its shade to everyone,
good and bad, young and old, high and low; to
animals and humans and every living creature—
even to the one who seeks to cut it down. So
this is the first quality of love: its indiscriminate
character. That is why we are exhorted to be
like God, "who makes his sun to shine on good
and bad alike and makes his rain to fall on

saints and sinners alike; so you must be all goodness as your heavenly Father is all goodness." Contemplate in astonishment the sheer goodness of the rose, the lamp, the tree, for there you have an image of what love is all about.

How does one attain this quality of love? Anything you *do* will only make it forced, cultivated and therefore phony, for love cannot be forced. There is nothing you can do. But there is something you can drop. Observe the marvelous change that comes over you the moment you stop seeing people as good and bad, as saints and sinners and begin to see them as unaware and ignorant. You must drop your false belief that people can sin in awareness. No one can sin in the light of awareness. Sin occurs, not, as we mistakenly think, in malice, but in ignorance. "Father, forgive them for they do not know what they are doing." To see this is to acquire the indiscriminate quality one so admires in the rose, the lamp and the tree.

And here is a second quality of love—its gratuitousness. Like the tree, the rose, the lamp, it gives and asks for nothing in return. How we despise the man whose choice of his wife is determined not by any quality she may have but by the amount of money she will bring as dowry. Such a man, we rightly say, loves not the woman but the financial benefit she brings him. But is your own love any different when you seek the company of those who bring you emotional gratification and avoid those who don't; when you are positively disposed toward people who give you what you want and live up to your expectations and are negative or indifferent toward those who don't? Here too there is only one thing that you need do to acquire this quality of gratuitousness that characterizes love. You can open your eyes and *see*. Just seeing, just exposing your so-called love for what it really is, a camouflage for selfishness and greed, is a major step toward arriving at this second quality of love.

The third quality of love is its unselfconsciousness. Love so enjoys the loving that it is blissfully unaware of itself. The way the lamp is busy shining with no thought of whether it is benefiting others or not. The way a rose gives out its fragrance simply because there is nothing else it can do, whether there is someone to enjoy the fragrance or not. The way the tree offers its shade. The light, the fragrance and the shade are not produced at the approach of persons and turned off when there is no one there. These things, like love, exist independently of persons. Love simply *is*, it has no object. They simply *are,* regardless of whether someone will benefit

from them or not. So they have no consciousness of any merit or of doing good. Their left
hand has no consciousness of what their right
hand does. "Lord, when did we see you hungry
or thirsty and help you?"

The final quality of love is its freedom. The
moment coercion or control or conflict enters,
love dies. Think how the rose, the tree, the lamp
leave you completely free. The tree will make no
effort to drag you into its shade if you are in
danger of a sunstroke. The lamp will not force
its light on you lest you stumble in the dark.
Think for a while of all the coercion and control
that you submit to on the part of others when
you so anxiously live up to their expectations in
order to buy their love and approval or because
you fear you will lose them. Each time you submit to this control and this coercion you destroy
the capacity to love which is your very nature,
for you cannot but do to others what you allow
others to do to you. Contemplate, then, all the
control and coercion in your life and hopefully
this contemplation alone will cause them to
drop. The moment they drop, freedom will
arise. And freedom is just another word for
love.

No Looking Back

NO ONE WHO PUTS HIS HAND TO THE PLOW
AND LOOKS BACK IS FIT FOR THE KINGDOM OF
GOD.

—LUKE 9:62

God's kingdom is love. What does it mean to love? It means to be sensitive to life, to things, to persons, to feel for everything and everyone to the exclusion of nothing and no one. For exclusion can only be achieved through a hardening of oneself, through closing one's doors. And the moment there is a hardening, sensitivity dies. It won't be hard for you to find examples of this kind of sensitivity in your life. Have you ever stopped to remove a stone or a nail from the road lest someone come to harm? It does not matter that you will never know the person who will benefit from this gesture and you will receive no reward or recognition. You just do it from a feeling of benevolence and kindness. Or have you felt pained at the wanton destruction in another part of the world, of a forest that you will never see and never benefit from? Have you gone to some trouble to help a stranger find his way though you do not know and will never meet this person again, purely from a good-heartedness that you feel within you? In these and so many other moments, love came to the surface in your life signaling that it was there within you waiting to be released.

How can you come to possess this kind of love? You cannot, because it is already there within you. All you have to do is remove the blocks you place to sensitivity and it would surface.

The blocks to sensitivity are two; Belief and Attachment. Belief—as soon as you have a belief you have come to a conclusion about a person or situation or thing. You have now become fixed and have dropped your sensitivity. You are prejudiced and will see the person from the eye of that prejudice. In other words, you will cease to see this person again. And how can you be sensitive to someone you do not even see? Take just one or two of your acquaintances and list the many positive or negative conclusions you have arrived at and on the basis of which you relate to her/him. The moment you say so-and-so is wise or is cruel or defensive or loving or whatever, you have hardened your perception and become prejudiced and ceased to perceive this person moment by moment, somewhat like a pilot who operates today with last week's weather report. Take a hard look at these beliefs, for the mere realization that they are beliefs, conclusions, prejudices, not reflections of reality, will cause them to drop.

Attachment—how is an attachment formed? First comes the contact with something that gives you pleasure: a car, an attractively advertised modern appliance, a word of praise, a person's company. Then comes the desire to hold on to it, to repeat the gratifying sensation that this thing or person caused you. Finally comes the conviction that you will not be happy without this person or thing, for you have equated the pleasure it brings you with happiness. You now have a full-blown attachment; and with it comes an inevitable exclusion of other things, an insensitivity to anything that isn't part of your attachment. Each time you leave the object of your attachment, you leave your heart there, so you cannot invest it in the next place you go to. The symphony of life moves on but you keep looking back, clinging to a few bars of the melody, blocking your ears to the rest of the music, thereby producing disharmony and conflict between what life is offering you and what you are clinging to. Then comes the tension and anxiety which are the very death of love and the joyful freedom that love brings. For love and freedom are only found when one enjoys each note as it arises, then allows it to go, so as to be fully receptive to the notes that follow.

How does one drop an attachment? People try to do this through renunciation. But to renounce some bars of the music, to blot them out of one's consciousness creates exactly the type of violence, conflict and insensitivity that clinging does. Once again you have hardened yourself. The secret is to renounce nothing, cling to nothing, enjoy everything and allow it to pass, to flow. How? Through many hours of observing the rottenness, the corrupt nature of an attachment. You generally concentrate on the thrill, the flash of pleasure that it brings. But contemplate the anxiety, the pain, the unfreedom; simultaneously contemplate the joy, the peace and freedom that are yours each time an attachment drops. Then you will stop looking back and allow yourself to be enchanted by the music of the present moment.

Finally take a look at this society we live in —rotten to the core, infected as it is with attachments. For if anyone is attached to power, money, property, to fame and success; if anyone seeks these things as if their happiness depended on them, they will be considered productive members of society, dynamic and hardworking. In other words, if they pursue these things with a driving ambition that destroys the symphony of their life and makes them hard and cold and insensitive to others and to themselves, society will look upon them as dependable citizens, and their relatives and friends will be proud of the status that they have achieved. How many so-called respectable people do you know who have retained the gentle sensitivity of love that only unattachment can offer? If you contemplate this long enough, you will experience a disgust so deep that you will instinctively fling every attachment away as you would a serpent that has settled on you. You will revolt and break loose from this putrid culture that is based on acquisitiveness and attachment, on anxiety and greed and on the hardness and insensitivity of nonlove.

Love Your Enemies

∽

But I say to you that hear, Love your
enemies, do good to those who hate you.

—Luke 6:27

When you are in love you find yourself looking
at everyone with new eyes; you become generous, forgiving, kindhearted, where before you
might have been hard and mean. Inevitably people begin reacting to you in the same way and
soon you find yourself living in a loving world
that you yourself have created. Or think of the
time you were in a bad mood and found yourself becoming irritable, mean, suspicious, even
paranoid. The next thing you knew everyone
was reacting to you in a negative way and you
found yourself living in a hostile world created
by your head and your emotions.

How could you go about creating a happy,
loving, peaceful world? By learning a simple,

beautiful, but painful art called the art of looking. This is how you do it: Every time you find
yourself irritated or angry with someone, the
one to look at is not that person but yourself.
The question to ask is not, "What's wrong with
this person?" but "What does this irritation tell
me about myself?" Do this right now. Think of
some irritating person you know and say this
painful but liberating sentence to yourself. "The
cause of my irritation is not in this person but in
me." Having said that, begin the task of finding
out how you are causing the irritation. First
look into the very real possibility that the reason
why this person's defects or so-called defects an-
noy you is that you have them yourself. But you
have repressed them and so are projecting them
unconsciously into the other. This is almost always true but hardly anyone recognizes it. So
search for this person's defects in your own
heart and in your unconscious mind, and your
annoyance will turn to gratitude that his or her
behavior has led you to self-discovery.

Here is something else worth looking at:
Can it be that you are annoyed at what this
person says or does because those words and
behavior are pointing out something in your life
and in yourself that you are refusing to see?
Think how irritated people become with the
mystic and the prophet who look far from mys-

tical or prophetical when we are challenged by their words or their life.

Another thing is also clear: You become irritated with this person because he/she is not living up to the expectations that have been programmed into you. Maybe you have a right to demand that he or she live up to your programming, as for instance, when he or she is cruel or unjust, but then stop to consider this. If you seek to change this person or to stop this person's behavior, will you not be more effective if you were not irritated? Irritation will only cloud your perception and make your action less effective. Everyone knows that when a sportsman or a boxer loses his temper, the quality of his play goes down because it becomes uncoordinated through passion and anger. In most cases, however, you have no right to demand that this person live up to your expectations; someone else in your place would be exposed to this behavior and would experience no annoyance at all. Just contemplate this truth and your irritation will vanish. How foolish of you to demand that someone else live up to standards and norms that your parents programmed into you!

And here is a final truth for you to consider: Given the background, the life experience, and the unawareness of this person, he cannot help behaving the way he does. It has been so well said that to understand all is to forgive all. If you really understood this person you would see him as crippled and not blameworthy, and your irritation would instantly cease. And the next thing you know you will be treating him/her with love, and he/she is responding with love and you find yourself living in a loving world which you have yourself created.

Tax Collectors and
Sinners

ॐ

The pharisees said to his disciples, "Why does your teacher eat with tax collectors and sinners?"

—Matthew 9:11

If you wish to get in touch with the reality of a thing, the first thing you must understand is that every idea distorts reality and is a barrier to seeing reality. The idea is not the reality, the idea "wine" is not wine, the idea "woman" is not this woman. If I really want to get in touch with the reality of this woman I must put aside my idea of womanness or Indianness and experience her in her thisness, her concreteness, her uniqueness. Unfortunately most people most of the time do not take the trouble to see things like this in their uniqueness; they just see the words or the ideas, they never look with the eyes of a child at this concrete, unique, fluffy, alive thing that is moving out there in front of them. They only see a sparrow, they never see the wondrous marvel of this unique human being here in front of them. They only see an Indian peasant woman. The idea therefore is a barrier to the perception of reality.

There is yet another barrier to the perception of reality—the judgment. This thing or person is good or bad, ugly or beautiful. It is barrier enough to have the idea of Indian or woman or peasant when I look at this concrete individual. But now I add a judgment and I say, "She is good," or "She is bad," or "She is attractive and beautiful," or "She is unattractive and ugly." That further prevents me from seeing her because she is neither good nor bad. She is "she" in all her uniqueness. The crocodile and the tiger are neither good nor bad, they are crocodile and tiger. Good and bad are in relation to something outside them. Inasmuch as they suit my purpose or please my eyes, or help me, or threaten me, I call them good or bad.

Now think of yourself when you were called good or attractive or beautiful by someone. Either you hardened yourself because you really thought you were ugly and you said to yourself, "If you really knew me as I am you would not call me beautiful." Or you opened yourself to the words of that person and you really thought that you were beautiful and you allowed yourself to be thrilled at the compliment. In both cases you were wrong, because you are neither beautiful nor ugly. You are *you*. If you get caught up in the judgments of people around you, you are eating the fruit of tension and insecurity and anxiety, because when today they call you beautiful and you are elated, tomorrow they will call you ugly and you will be depressed. Therefore the proper and accurate response when someone calls you beautiful is to say, "This person given his present perception and mood sees me as beautiful, but that does not say anything about me. Someone else in his place and depending on his background and mood and perception will see me as ugly. But that again says nothing about me."

How easily we are taken in by the judgment of other people and then form an image of ourselves based on this judgment. In order to be truly liberated you need to listen to the so-called good and bad things that they tell you, but to feel no emotion at the feedback any more than a computer does when data is fed into it. Because what they say about you reveals more about them than about you.

As a matter of fact you also have to be aware of the judgments that you make about yourself, because even those are generally based

~

on the value systems that you picked up from the people around you. If you judge, condemn, approve, do you ever see reality? If you look at anything through the eye of judgment or approval or condemnation, is that not the major barrier to understanding and observing things as they are in themselves? Take the time when somebody told you that you are very special to him; if you accepted that compliment then you ate the fruit of tension. Why do you want to be special to someone and to submit to that kind of approval and judgment? Why not just be content to be you?

When someone tells you how special you are, all that you can accurately say is: This person given his particular taste and needs, desires, appetites and projections has a special desire for me, but that says nothing about me as a person. Someone else will find me quite unspecial and that too says nothing about me as a person. So the moment you accept that compliment and you allow yourself to enjoy it, you will give control of yourself to that person. You will go to great lengths in order to continue to be special to this person. You will be in constant fear lest he meets someone who will become special to him and thus you will be dislodged from the special position you occupy in his life. And you will be constantly dancing to his tunes, living up to his expectations, and in doing so you will have lost your freedom. You have made yourself dependent on him for your happiness, for you have made your happiness depend on his judgment of you.

Then you can make things worse by beginning to search for other people who will tell you that you are special to them and you invest so much time and energy in making sure that they never lose this image they have of you. What a wearisome way to live! Suddenly fear comes into your life, fear that the image will be destroyed, and if what you seek is fearlessness and freedom, you must let go of this. How? By refusing to take anybody seriously when they tell you how special you are. The words "You are special to me" simply say something about my present mood regarding you, my taste, my present state of mind and development. They say nothing else. So accept that as a fact and do not rejoice in it. What you may rejoice in is my company and not my compliment. What you may enjoy is my present interaction with you, not my praise. And if you are wise, you will urge me to find many other special people so that you are never tempted to hold on to this image that I have of you. It is not my image of you that you enjoy because you are ceaselessly aware that my image of you can change so easily. So what you enjoy is the present moment, because if you enjoy the image that I have of you, I will control you and you will be afraid to be yourself lest you hurt me, you will be afraid to tell me the truth, to do or say anything that would damage the image that I have of you.

Apply this now to every image that people have of you and they tell you that you are a genius or wise or good or holy, and you enjoy that compliment and in that minute you lose your freedom; because now you will be constantly striving to retain that opinion. You will fear to make mistakes, to be yourself, to do or say anything that will spoil the image. You have lost the freedom to make a fool of yourself, to be laughed at and to be ridiculed, to do and say whatever feels right to you rather than what fits in with the image others have of you. How does one break this? Through many patient hours of study, awareness, observation, of what this silly image brings you. It gives you a thrill combined with so much insecurity and unfreedom and suffering. If you were to see this clearly you would lose your appetite to be special to anyone, or to be highly regarded by anyone. You would move about with sinners or bad characters and do and say as you please, regardless of what people think of you. You would become like the birds and flowers that are so totally unselfconscious, too busy with the task of living to care one little bit about what others think of them, about whether they are special to others or not. And at last, you will have become fearless and free.

Be Awake

Blessed are those servants whom the master finds awake when he comes.

—Luke 12:37

Everywhere in the world people are in search of love, for everyone is convinced that love alone can save the world, love alone can make life meaningful and worth living. But how very few understand what love really is, and how it arises in the human heart. It is so frequently equated with good feelings toward others, with benevolence or nonviolence or service. But these things in themselves are not love. Love springs from awareness. It is only inasmuch as you see someone as he or she really is here and now and not as they are in your memory or your desire or in your imagination or projection that you can truly love them, otherwise it is not the person that you love but the idea that you have formed of this person, or this person as the object of your desire not as he or she is in themselves.

Therefore the first act of love is to see this person or this object, this reality as it truly is. And this involves the enormous discipline of dropping your desires, your prejudices, your memories, your projections, your selective way of looking, a discipline so great that most people would rather plunge headlong into good actions and service than submit to the burning fire of this asceticism. When you set out to serve someone whom you have not taken the trouble to see, are you meeting that person's need or your own? So the first ingredient of love is to really see the other.

The second ingredient is equally important to see yourself, to ruthlessly flash the light of awareness on your motives, your emotions, your needs, your dishonesty, your self-seeking, your tendency to control and manipulate. This means calling things by their name, no matter how painful the discovery and the consequences. If you achieve this kind of awareness of the other and yourself, you will know what love is. For you will have attained a mind and a heart that is alert, vigilant, clear, sensitive, a clarity of perception, a sensitivity that will draw out of you an accurate, appropriate response to every situation at every moment. Sometimes you will be irresistibly impelled into action, at others you will be held back and restrained. You will sometimes be made to ignore others and sometimes give them the attention they seek. At times you will be gentle and yielding, at others hard, uncompromising, assertive, even violent. For the love that is born of sensitivity takes many unexpected forms and it responds not to prefabricated guidelines and principles but to present, concrete reality. When you first experience this kind of sensitivity you are likely to experience terror. For all your defenses will be torn down, your dishonesty exposed, the protected walls around you burned.

Think of the terror that comes to a rich man when he sets out to really see the pitiful condition of the poor, to a power-hungry dictator when he really looks at the plight of the people he oppresses, to a fanatic, a bigot, when he really sees the falsehood of his convictions when they do not fit the facts. The terror that comes to the romantic lover when he decides to really see that what he loves is not his beloved but his image of her. That is why the most painful act the human being can perform, the act that he dreads the most is the act of seeing. It is in that act of seeing that love is born, or rather more accurately, that act of seeing is Love.

Once you begin to see, your sensitivity will drive you to the awareness, not just of the things that you choose to see but of everything else as well. Your poor ego will try desperately to blunt that sensitivity because its defenses are being stripped away and it is left with no protection and nothing to cling to. If you ever allow yourself to see it will be the death of you. And that is why love is so terrifying, for to love is to see and to see is to die. But it is also the most delightful exhilarating experience in the whole world. For in the death of the ego is freedom, peace, serenity, joy.

If it is love that you truly desire then set out at once on the task of seeing, take it seriously and look at someone you dislike and really see your prejudice. Look at someone you cling to or something you cling to and really see the suffering, the futility, the unfreedom of clinging and look long and lovingly at human faces and human behavior. Take some time out to gaze in wonder at Nature, the flight of a bird, a flower in bloom, the dry leaf crumbling to dust, the flow of a river, the rising of the moon, a silhouette of a mountain against the sky. And as you do this the hard, protective shell around your heart will soften and melt and your heart will come alive in sensitivity and responsiveness. The darkness in your eyes will be dispelled and your vision will become clear and penetrating, and you will know at last what love is.

THE MOUNTAIN OF PRAYER

∽

AND AFTER HE HAD DISMISSED THE CROWDS,
HE WENT UP ON THE MOUNTAIN BY HIMSELF
TO PRAY.

—MATTHEW 14:23

Has it ever occurred to you that you can only love when you are alone? What does it mean to love? It means to see a person, a thing, a situation, as it really is and not as you imagine it to be, and to give it the response it deserves. You cannot love what you do not even see.

And what prevents you from seeing? Your concepts, your categories, your prejudices and projections, your needs and attachments, the labels you have drawn from your conditioning and from your past experiences. Seeing is the most arduous thing a human being can undertake. For it calls for a disciplined, alert mind, whereas most people would much rather lapse into mental laziness than take the trouble to see each person and thing anew in present-moment freshness.

To drop your conditioning in order to see is arduous enough. But seeing calls for something more painful still. The dropping of the control that society exercises over you; a control whose tentacles have penetrated to the very roots of your being, so that to drop it is to tear yourself apart.

If you wish to understand this, think of a little child that is given a taste for drugs. As the drug penetrates the body of the child, it becomes addicted and its whole being cries out for the drug. To be without the drug is so unbearable a torment that it seems preferable to die.

Now this is exactly what society did to you when you were a child. You were not allowed to enjoy the solid, nutritious food of life: work and play and the company of people and the pleasures of the senses and the mind. You were given a taste for the drug called Approval, Appreciation, Attention, the drug called Success, Prestige, Power. Having got a taste for these things you became addicted and began to dread their loss. You felt terror at the prospect of failure, of mistakes, of the criticism of others. So you became cravenly dependent on people and lost your freedom. Others now have the power to make you happy or miserable. And much as you now hate the suffering this involves, you find yourself completely helpless. There is never a minute when, consciously or unconsciously, you are not attuned to the reaction of others, marching to the drum of their demands. When you are ignored or disapproved of, you experience a loneliness so unbearable that you crawl back to people to beg for the comfort known as Support, Encouragement, Reassurance. To live with people in this state involves never-ending tension; but to live without them brings the agony of loneliness. You have lost your capacity to see them clearly as they are and to respond to them accurately because mostly your perception of them is clouded by your need to get your drug.

The consequence of all this is terrifying and inescapable: You have become incapable of loving anyone or anything. If you wish to love you must learn to see again. And if you wish to see you must give up your drug. You must tear away from your being the roots of society that have penetrated to the marrow. You must drop out. Externally everything will go on as before, you will continue to be in the world, but no longer of it. And in your heart you will now be free at last and utterly alone. It is only in this aloneness, this utter solitude, that dependence and desire will die, and the capacity to love is born. For one no longer sees others as means to satisfy one's addiction.

Only someone who has attempted this knows the terror of the process. It is like inviting yourself to die. It is like asking the poor drug addict to give up the only happiness he has known and to replace it with a taste for bread and fruit and the clean fresh morning air and the sweetness of the water from the mountain stream, while he is struggling to cope with his withdrawal symptoms and with the emptiness that he experiences within himself now that his drug has gone. To his fevered mind nothing can fill the emptiness except his drug. Can you imagine a life in which you refuse to enjoy a single word of approval and appreciation, or to lean on someone's arm; in which you depend on no one emotionally, so no one has the power to make you happy or miserable anymore; you refuse to need any particular person or to be special to anyone or to call anyone your own? Even the birds of the air have their nests and the foxes their holes, but you will have nowhere to rest your head in your journey through life.

If you ever get to this state you will at last know what it means to see with a vision that is clear and unclouded by fear or desire. And you will know what it means to love. But to come to this land of love you have to pass through the pains of death. For to love persons is to have died to the need for persons and to be utterly alone.

How would you ever get there? By ceaseless awareness, and the infinite patience and compassion that you would have for a drug addict. It will also help you to undertake activities that you can do with your whole being, activities that you so much love to do, that while you are engaged in them, success or recognition or approval simply do not mean a thing to you. It will help too if you return to Nature: Send the crowds away and go up into the mountain and silently commune with trees and flowers and animals and birds, with sea and sky and clouds and stars. Then you will know that your heart has brought you into the vast desert of solitude. There is no one there by your side, absolutely no one. At first it will seem unbearable, but that is only because you are unaccustomed to aloneness. But if you manage to stay there for a while the desert will suddenly blossom into Love. Your heart will burst into song. And it will be springtime forever.

Judge Not

☙

JUDGE NOT, THAT YOU BE NOT JUDGED.

—MATTHEW 7:1

It is a sobering thought that the finest act of love you can perform is not an act of service but an act of contemplation, of seeing. When you serve people you help, support, comfort, alleviate pain. When you see them in their inner beauty and goodness you transform and create.

Think of some of the people you like and are drawn to you. Now attempt to look at each of them as if you were seeing them for the first time, not allowing yourself to be influenced by your past knowledge or experience of them, whether good or bad. Look for things in them that you may have missed because of familiarity, for familiarity breeds staleness, blindness and boredom. You cannot love what you cannot see afresh. You cannot love what you are not constantly discovering anew.

Having done this move on now to people you dislike. First observe what it is in them that you dislike, study their defects impartially and with detachment. That means you cannot use labels like proud, lazy, selfish, arrogant. The label is an act of mental laziness, for it is easy to stick a label onto someone. It is difficult and challenging to see this person in his/her uniqueness.

You must study those defects clinically, that means, you must first make sure of your objectivity. Consider the possibility that what you see as a defect in them may not be a defect at all but really something that your upbringing and conditioning have led you to dislike. If after this you still see a defect there, understand that the origin of the defect lies in childhood experiences, past conditionings, faulty thinking and perception; and above all in unawareness, not in malice. As you do this your attitude will change into love and forgiveness, for to study, to observe, to understand is to forgive.

Having made this study of defects, now search for the treasures buried in this person that your dislike prevented you from seeing before. And as you do this observe any change of attitude or feeling that comes over you, for your dislike had clouded the vision and prevented you from seeing.

You can now move on to each of the persons you live and work with, observing how each of them becomes transformed in your eyes when you look at them in this way. In seeing them thus it is an infinitely more loving gift that you offer them than any act of service. For in doing this you have transformed them, you have created them in your heart and, given a certain amount of contact between you and them, they will be transformed in reality too.

Now make this same gift to yourself. If you have been able to do it for others that should be fairly easy. Follow the same procedure: No defect, no neurosis is judged or condemned. You have not judged others, you will be amazed now that you yourself are not being judged. Those defects are probed, studied, analyzed, for a better understanding that leads to love and forgiveness, and you will discover to your joy that you are being transformed by this strangely loving attitude that arises within you toward this thing you call yourself. An attitude that arises within you and moves out through you to every living creature.

Pluck Out the Eye

⁓

AND IF YOUR HAND CAUSES YOU TO SIN, CUT
IT OFF, IT IS BETTER TO ENTER LIFE MAIMED
THAN WITH TWO HANDS TO GO TO HELL . . .
AND IF YOUR EYE CAUSES YOU TO SIN, PLUCK
IT OUT; IT IS BETTER FOR YOU TO ENTER THE
KINGDOM OF GOD WITH ONE EYE THAN WITH
TWO EYES TO BE THROWN INTO HELL.

—MARK 9:43ff.

When you deal with blind people it dawns on
you that they are attuned to realities that you
have no idea of. Their sensitivity to the world of
touch and smell and taste and sound is such, as
to make the rest of us seem like dull clods. We
pity persons who have lost their sight but rarely
take into account the enrichment that their
other senses offer them. It is a pity that those
riches are bought at the heavy price of blindness
and it is quite conceivable that we could be as
alive and finely attuned to the world as blind
people are without the loss of our eyes. But it is
not possible, not even conceivable, that you
would ever awaken to the world of love unless

you pluck out, chop off, those parts of your psychological being that are called Attachments.

If you refuse to do this you will miss the experience of love, you miss the only thing that gives meaning to human existence. For love is the passport to abiding joy and peace and freedom. There is only one thing that blocks out entry into that world and the name of that thing is Attachment. It is produced by the lusting eye that excites craving within the heart and by the grasping hand that reaches out to hold, possess and make one's own, and refuses to let go. It is this eye that must be gouged out, this hand that must be cut off if love is to be born. With those mutilated stumps for hands you can grasp nothing anymore. With those empty sockets for eyes you suddenly become sensitive to realities whose existence you have never suspected.

Now at last you can love, till now all you had was a certain good-heartedness and benevolence, a sympathy and concern for others, which you mistakenly took for love but has as little in common with love, as a flickering candle flame has with the light of the sun.

What is love? It is a sensitivity to every portion of reality within you and without, together with a wholehearted response to that reality. Sometimes you will embrace that reality, sometimes you will attack it, sometimes you will ignore it and at others you will give it your fullest attention, but always you will respond not from need but from sensitivity.

And what is an attachment? A need, a clinging that blunts your sensitivity, a drug that clouds your perception. That is why as long as you have the slightest attachment for anything or any person, love cannot be born. For love is sensitivity, and sensitivity that is impaired even in the slightest degree is sensitivity destroyed. Just as the malfunctioning of one essential piece of a radar set distorts reception, and distorts your response to what you perceive.

There is no such thing as defective love, or deficient love, or partial love. Love like sensitivity either is in all its fullness or it simply is not. You either have it whole or you have it not. So it is only when attachments disappear that one enters the boundless realm of spiritual freedom called love. One is now released to see and to respond. But you must not confound this freedom with the indifference of those who have never passed through the stage of attachment. How could you pluck out an eye or amputate a hand that you do not have? This indifference that so many people mistake for love (because they are attached to no one, they think that they love everyone) is not sensitivity, but a hardening of the heart that has come about from rejection or disillusionment or the practice of renunciation.

No, one must brave the stormy seas of attachments if one has to arrive at the land of love. Some people never having set sail have convinced themselves that they have arrived. One must be able-bodied and clear-sighted before the sword can do its work and the world of love can arise in one's awareness; and make no mistake, this is only achieved through violence. It is only the violent who carry off the kingdom.

Why the violence? Because left to its own devices life would never produce love, it would only lead you to attraction, from attraction to pleasure, then to attachment, to satisfaction, which finally leads to wearisomeness and boredom. Then comes a plateau. Then once again the weary cycle: attraction, pleasure, attachment, fulfillment, satisfaction, boredom. All of this mixed with the anxieties, the jealousies, the possessiveness, the sorrow, the pain, that make the cycle a roller coaster.

When you have gone repeatedly around and around the cycle, a time finally comes when you have had enough and want to call a halt to the whole process. And if you are lucky enough not to run into something or someone else that catches your eye, you will have at least attained a fragile peace. That is the most that life can give you; and you can mistakenly equate this state with freedom and you die without ever having known what it means to be really free and to love.

No, if you wish to break out of the cycle and into the world of love, you must strike while the attachment is alive and raw, not when you have outgrown it. And you must strike not with the sword of renunciation, for that kind of mutilation only hardens, but with the sword of awareness.

What must you be aware of? Three things: First, you must see the suffering that this drug is causing you, the ups and downs, the thrills, the anxieties and disappointments, the boredom to which it must inevitably lead. Second, you must realize what this drug is cheating you out of, namely, the freedom to love and to enjoy every minute and everything in life. Third, you must understand how, because of your addiction and your programming, you have invested the object of your attachment with a beauty and a value it simply does not have: What you are so enamored of is in your head, not in your beloved person or thing. See this and the sword of awareness breaks the spell.

It is commonly held that it is only when you feel deeply loved yourself, that you are able to go out in love to others. This is not true. A man in love does indeed go out to the world not in love but in euphoria. For him the world takes on an unreal, rosy hue, which it loses the moment the euphoria dies. His so-called love is generated not by his clear perception of reality but by the conviction, true or false, that he is loved by someone—a conviction that is dangerously fragile, because it is founded on the unreliable, changeable people who he believes love him. And who can at any moment pull the switch and turn off his euphoria. No wonder those who walk this path never really lose their insecurity.

(When you go out to the world because of the love that someone else has for you, you are all aglow not with your perception of reality but with the love that you have received from someone else; someone else controls the switch and when it is switched off the glow fades away.)

As you use the sword of awareness to move from attachment into love, there is one thing you must keep in mind: Don't be harsh or impatient, or hating of yourself. How can love grow out of such attitudes? But rather hold on to the compassion and the matter-of-factness with which the surgeon plies his knife. Then you may find yourself in the marvelous condition of loving the object of your attachment and enjoying it even more than before, but simultaneously enjoying every other thing and every other person just as much.

That is the litmus test for finding out if what you have is love. Far from becoming indifferent, you now enjoy everything and everyone just as much as you did the object of your attachment. Only now there are no more thrills and therefore no more suffering and suspense. In fact you could be said to be enjoying everything and enjoying nothing. Because you have made the great discovery that what you are enjoying on the occasion of each thing and person is something within yourself. The orchestra is within you and you carry it with you wherever you go. The things and people outside you merely determine what particular melody the orchestra will play. And when there is no one or nothing that has your attention the orchestra will play a music of its own; it needs no outside stimulation. You now carry in your heart a happiness that nothing outside of you can put there, and nothing can take away.

Here then is the other test of love. You are happy for no reason that you know. Does this love last? There is no guarantee that it does. For while love cannot be partial it can be of temporary duration. It comes and goes in the measure that your mind is awake and aware or has gone off to sleep again. But this much is certain, once you have had even a fleeting taste of this thing called love, you will know that no price is too high, no sacrifice too great, not even the loss of one's eyes, nor the computations of one's hand, if you can have in exchange the only thing in the world that makes your life worthwhile.

SUFFERING AND GLORY

❧

WAS IT NOT NECESSARY THAT THE CHRIST
SHOULD SUFFER THESE THINGS AND ENTER
INTO HIS GLORY?

—LUKE 24:26

Think of some of the painful events in your life.
For how many of them are you grateful today,
because thanks to them you changed and grew?
Here is a simple truth of life that most people
never discover. Happy events make life delightful but they do not lead to self-discovery and
growth and freedom. That privilege is reserved
to the things and persons and situations that
cause us pain.

Every painful event contains in itself a seed
of growth and liberation. In the light of this
truth return to your life now and take a look at
one or another of the events that you are not
grateful for, and see if you can discover the po-
tential for growth that they contain which you

were unaware of and therefore failed to benefit from. Now think of some recent event that caused you pain, that produced negative feelings in you. Whoever or whatever caused those feelings was your teacher, because they revealed so much to you about yourself that you probably did not know. And they offered you an invitation and a challenge to self-understanding, self-discovery, and therefore to growth and life and freedom.

Try it out now, identify the negative feeling that this event aroused in you. Was it anxiety or insecurity, jealousy or anger or guilt? What does that emotion say to you about yourself, your values, your way of perceiving the world and life and above all your programming and conditioning? If you succeed in discovering this, you will drop some illusion you have clung to till now, or you will change a distorted perception or correct a false belief or learn to distance yourself from your suffering, as you realize that it was caused by your programming and not by reality; and you will suddenly find that you are full of gratitude for those negative feelings and to that person or event that caused them.

Now take this one step further. Look at everything that you think and feel and say and do that you do not like in yourself. Your negative emotions, your defects, your handicaps, your errors, your attachments and neuroses and hang-ups and yes, even your sins. Can you see every one of them as a necessary part of your development, holding out a promise of growth and grace for you and others, that would never have been there except for this thing that you so disliked? And if you have caused pain and negative feelings to others, were you not at that moment a teacher to them, an instrument that offered them a seed for self-discovery and growth? Can you persist in this observation, in your observation till you see all of this as a happy fault, a necessary sin that brings so much good to you and to the world?

If you can, your heart will be flooded with peace and gratitude and love and acceptance of every single thing. And you will have discovered what people everywhere are searching for and never find. Namely, the fountainhead of serenity and joy that hides in every human heart.

FIRE ON THE EARTH

∽

I CAME TO CAST FIRE UPON THE EARTH; AND
WOULD THAT IT WERE ALREADY KINDLED!

—LUKE 12:49

If you want to know what it means to be happy,
look at a flower, a bird, a child; they are perfect
images of the kingdom. For they live from moment to moment in the eternal now with no past
and no future. So they are spared the guilt and
the anxiety that so torment human beings and
they are full of the sheer joy of living, taking
delight not so much in persons or things as in
life itself. As long as your happiness is caused or
sustained by something or someone outside of
you, you are still in the land of the dead. The
day you are happy for no reason whatsoever,
the day you find yourself taking delight in everything and in nothing, you will know that you

have found the land of unending joy called the kingdom.

To find the kingdom is the easiest thing in the world but also the most difficult. Easy because it is all around you and within you, and all you have to do is reach out and take possession of it. Difficult because if you wish to possess the kingdom you may possess nothing else. That is, you must drop all inward leaning on any person or thing, withdrawing from them forever the power to thrill you, or excite you, or to give you a feeling of security or well-being. For this you first need to see with unflinching clarity this simple and shattering truth: Contrary to what your culture and religion have taught you, nothing, but absolutely nothing can make you happy. The moment you see that, you will stop moving from one job to another, one friend to another, one place, one spiritual technique, one guru to another. None of these things can give you a single minute of happiness. They can only offer you a temporary thrill, a pleasure that initially grows in intensity, then turns into pain if you lose them and into boredom if you keep them.

Think of the numberless persons and things that so excited you in the past. What happened? In every single instance they ended up by causing you suffering, or boredom, did they not? It is absolutely essential that you see this because till you do, there is no question of your ever finding the kingdom of joy. Mostly people are not prepared to see till they have suffered repeated disillusionment and sorrow. And even then only one in a million has the desire to see. They just keep going at it pathetically knocking at the door of other creatures, begging bowl in hand, craving affection and approval and guidance and power and honor and success. For they obstinately refuse to understand that happiness is not in these things.

If you search within your heart you will find something there that will make it possible for you to understand: a spark of disenchantment and discontent, which if fanned into flame will become a raging forest fire that will burn up the whole of the illusory world you are living in, thereby unveiling to your wondering eyes the kingdom that you have always lived in unsuspectingly. Have you ever felt disgusted with life, sick at heart of constantly running away from fears and anxieties, weary of your begging rounds, exhausted from being dragged about helplessly by your attachments and addictions? Have you ever felt the utter meaninglessness of working for a degree, then finding a job, then settling down to a life of boredom; or, if you are an achiever, settling down to a life of emotional turmoil caused by the things that you are chasing after? If you have, and is there a single human being who hasn't, the divine flame of discontent has arisen within your heart. Now is the time to feed it before it gets stamped out by the routine chores of life. Now is the Holy Season when you simply must find the time to get away and look at your life, allowing the flame to grow and grow as you look, refusing to let anything distract you from this task.

Now is the time to see that absolutely nothing outside of you can bring you lasting joy. But the moment you do that you will notice that a fear arises in your heart. That fear that if you allow the discontent to be, it will turn into a raging passion that will grip you and cause you to revolt against everything that your culture and your religion hold dear; against a whole way of thinking and feeling and perceiving the world that they have brainwashed you into accepting. This devouring flame will cause you not just to rock the boat but to burn the boat to ashes. Suddenly you will find yourself living in an altogether different world, infinitely removed from the world of the people around you, for everything that others hold dear, everything they are crying their hearts out for, honor, power, acceptance, approval, security, wealth, is seen for the stinking garbage that it is. It disgusts and nauseates. And everything others are forever running away from holds no terrors for you anymore. You have become serene and fearless and free, for you have stepped out of your illusory world and into the kingdom.

Do not confound this divine discontent with the hopelessness and despair that sometimes drive people to madness and to suicide. That is not the mystical drive to life but the neurotic drive to self-destruction. Do not confound it with the whining of people who are forever complaining about everything. These people are not mystics but bores merely agitating for improvement of prison conditions whereas what they need to do is burst out of prison into freedom.

Most people when they feel the stirring of this discontent within their hearts either run away from it and drug themselves with the fevered pursuit of work and social life and friendship; or they channelize the discontent into social work, literature, music, the so-called creative pursuits that make them settle for reform, when what is needed is revolt. These people even though they are full of activity are not really alive at all: They are dead, content to live in the land of the dead. The test that your discontent is divine is the fact that it has no trace of sadness or bitterness to it at all. On the contrary even though it often arouses fear within your heart, it is always accompanied by joy, the joy of the kingdom.

And here is a parable of that kingdom: It is like a treasure lying buried in a field. The man who found it buried it again, and for sheer joy went and sold everything he had and bought that field. If you haven't found the treasure as yet, don't waste your time searching for it. It can be found but it may not be searched for. You don't have the slightest notion what the treasure is. All you are familiar with is the drugged happiness of your present existence. So what would you search for? And where? No, search rather in your heart for the spark of discontent and tend the flame till it becomes a conflagration and your world is burned down to a heap of rubble.

Young or old, most of us are discontented merely because we want something—more knowledge, a better job, a finer car, a bigger salary. Our discontent is based upon our desire for "the more." It is only because we want something more that most of us are discontented. But I am not talking about that kind of discontent. It is the desire for "the more" that prevents clear thinking, whereas if we are discontented, not because we want something, but without knowing what we want; if we are dissatisfied with our jobs, with making money, with seeking position and power, with tradition, with what we have and with what we might have; if we are dissatisfied, not with anything in particular but with everything, then I think we shall find that our discontent brings clarity. When we don't accept or follow, but question, investigate, penetrate, there is an insight out of which comes creativity, joy.

Mostly the discontent that you feel comes from not having enough of something—you are dissatisfied because you think you do not have enough money or power or success or fame or virtue or love, or holiness. This is not the discontent that leads to the joy of the kingdom. Its source is greed and ambition and its fruit is restlessness and frustration. The day you are discontented not because you want more of something but without knowing what it is you want; when you are sick at heart of everything that you have been pursuing so far and you are sick of the pursuit itself, then your heart will attain a great clarity, an insight that will cause you mysteriously to delight in everything and in nothing.

CONSIDER THE LILIES

॰ॐ॰

THEREFORE I TELL YOU, DO NOT BE ANXIOUS
ABOUT YOUR LIFE . . . LOOK AT THE BIRDS OF
THE AIR . . . CONSIDER THE LILIES OF THE
FIELD . . .

—MATTHEW 6:25ff.

Everyone at some time or the other experiences
feelings of what is known as insecurity. You feel
insecure with the amount of money you have in
the bank, or the amount of love you are getting
from your friend or the type of educational
background you have had. Or you have insecurity feelings regarding your health or your age
or your physical appearance. If you were asked
the question, "What is it that makes you feel
insecure?" you would almost certainly give the
wrong answer. You might say, "I don't have
enough of the love of a friend" or "I don't have
the kind of academic training that I need," or
some such thing. In other words, you would
point to some outside condition not realizing

that insecurity feelings are not generated by anything outside of you, but only by your emotional programming, by something you are telling yourself in your head. If you change your program, your insecurity feelings would vanish in a second, even though everything in the outside world remained exactly as it was before. One person feels quite secure with practically no money in the bank, another feels insecure even though he has millions. It isn't the amount of money but their programming that makes the difference. One person has no friends, yet feels perfectly secure in the love of people. Another feels insecure even in the most possessive and exclusive of relationships. Again the difference is in the programming.

If you wish to deal with your feelings of insecurity there are four facts that you must study well and understand. First, it is futile to ease your insecurity feelings by trying to change things outside of you. Your efforts may be successful, though mostly they are not. They may bring some relief, but the relief will be short-lived. So it is not worth the energy and time you spend in improving your physical appearance or making more money or getting further reassurances of love from your friends.

Second, this fact will lead you to tackle the problem where it really is, inside your head.

Think of the people who in exactly the same condition that you find yourself in now would not feel the slightest insecurity. There are such people. Therefore the problem lies not with reality outside of you but with you, in your programming.

Third, you must understand that this programming of yours was picked up from insecure people who, when you were very young and impressionable, taught you by their behavior and their panic reactions that every time the outside world did not conform to a certain pattern, you must create an emotional turmoil within yourself called insecurity. And you must do everything in your power to rearrange the outside world—make more money, seek more reassurances, placate and please the people you have offended, etc., etc.—in order to make the insecurity feelings go away. The mere realization that you don't have to do this, that doing this really solves nothing, and that the emotional turmoil is caused solely by you and your culture —this realization alone distances you from the problem and brings considerable relief.

Fourth, whenever you are insecure about what may happen in the future, just remember this: In the past six months or one year you were so insecure about events which when they finally came you were able to handle somehow.

Thanks to the energy and the resources that that particular present moment gave you, and not to all the previous worrying which only made you suffer needlessly and weakened you emotionally. So, say to yourself: "If there is anything I can do about the future, right now, I shall do it. Then I'm going to just leave it alone and settle down to enjoy the present moment, because all the experience of my life has shown me that I can only cope with things when they are present, not before they occur. And that the present always gives me the resources and the energy I need to deal with them."

The final disappearance of insecurity feelings will only come when you have attained that blessed ability of the birds of the air and the flowers of the field to live fully in the present, one moment at a time. The present moment, no matter how painful, is never unbearable. What is unbearable is what you think is going to happen in five hours or in five days; and those words you keep saying in your head, words like, "This is terrible, this is unbearable, how long is this going to last," and so on. Birds and flowers are blessed above humans in that they have no concept of the future, no words in their heads, and no anxiety about what their fellows think of them. That is why they are such perfect images of the kingdom. So do not be anxious about tomorrow, tomorrow will look after it-self. Each day has troubles enough of its own. Set your mind on God's kingdom before every-thing else and all the rest will come to you as well.

LOST AND FOUND

HE WHO FINDS HIS LIFE WILL LOSE IT, AND HE
WHO LOSES HIS LIFE FOR MY SAKE WILL FIND
IT.

—MATTHEW 10:39

Has it ever struck you that those who most fear
to die are the ones who most fear to live? That
in running away from death we are running
away from life?

Think of a man living in an attic, a little hole
of a place with no light and little ventilation. He
fears to come down the stairs because he has
heard of people falling downstairs and breaking
their necks. He would never cross a street because he has heard of thousands who have been
run over on the streets. And of course, if he cannot cross a street, how will he cross an ocean or
a continent or one world of ideas to another?
This man clings to his hole of an attic in the

∽

attempt to ward off death and in doing so he has simultaneously warded off life.

What is death? A loss, a disappearance, a letting go, a saying good-bye. When you cling you refuse to let go, you refuse to say good-bye, you resist death. And even though you may not realize it, that is when you resist life too.

For life is on the move and you are stuck, life flows and you have become stagnant, life is flexible and free and you are rigid and frozen. Life carries all things away and you crave for stability and permanence.

So you fear life and you fear death because you cling. When you cling to nothing, when you have no fear of losing anything, then you are free to flow like the mountain stream that is always fresh and sparkling and alive.

There are people who cannot bear the thought of losing a relative or a friend, they prefer not to think of it; or they dread to challenge and lose a pet theory or ideology or belief; or they are convinced that they are never able to live without this or that precious person, place or thing.

Do you want a way to measure the degree of your rigidity and your deadness? Observe the amount of pain you experience when you lose a cherished idea or person or thing. The pain and the grief betray your clinging, do they not? Why is it you grieve so much at the death of a loved one or the loss of a friend? You never took the time to seriously consider that all things change and pass away and die.

So death and loss and separation take you by surprise. You choose to live in a little attic of your illusion pretending that things will never change, that things will always be the same. That is why when life bursts in to shatter your illusion you experience so much pain.

In order to live you must look reality in the face and then you will shed your fear of losing people and develop a taste for newness and change and uncertainty. You will shed your fear of losing the known and expectantly wait and welcome the unfamiliar and the unknown. If it is life you seek then here is an exercise that might prove painful but will bring the exhilaration of freedom if you are able to do it.

Ask yourself if there is anything or anyone whose loss would cause you grief. You may be one of those persons who cannot bear to even think of the death or the loss of a parent, a friend, a loved one. If this is so, and in the measure that this is so, you are dead. The thing to do is to face the death, the loss, the separation, from loved things and loved ones now.

Take these persons and things one at a time and imagine they are dead or lost or separated from you forever, and in your heart say good-bye. To each of them say thank you and good-bye.

You will experience pain and you will experience the disappearance of clinging; and then something else will emerge in your consciousness, an aloneness, a solitude, that grows and grows and becomes like the infinite vastness of the sky. In that aloneness is freedom. In that solitude is life. In that nonclinging is the willingness to flow and to enjoy and to taste and to relish each new moment of life which is now made all the sweeter because it is freed from the anxiety and tension and insecurity, freed from the fear of loss and death that always accompanies the desire for permanence and clinging.

THE LAMP OF THE BODY

∽

YOUR EYE IS THE LAMP OF YOUR BODY; WHEN
YOUR EYE IS SOUND, YOUR WHOLE BODY IS
FULL OF LIGHT; BUT WHEN IT IS NOT SOUND,
YOUR BODY IS FULL OF DARKNESS.

—LUKE 11:34

We think the world would be saved if only we
could generate larger quantities of goodwill and
tolerance. That's false. What will save the world
is not goodwill and tolerance but clear thinking.
Of what use is it to be tolerant of others if you
are convinced that you are right and everyone
who disagrees with you is wrong? That isn't tolerance but condescension. That leads not to
union of hearts but to division, because you are
one up and the others one down. A position
that can only lead to a sense of superiority on
your part and resentment on your neighbor's,
thereby breeding further intolerance.

True tolerance only arises from a keen
awareness of the abysmal ignorance of everyone

as far as truth is concerned. For truth is essentially mystery. The mind can sense but cannot grasp it, much less formulate it. Our beliefs can point to it but cannot put it into words. In spite of this, people talk glowingly about the value of dialogue which at worst is a camouflaged attempt to convince the other person of the rightness of your position and at best will prevent you from becoming a frog in the well who thinks that his well is the only world there is.

What happens when frogs from different wells assemble to dialogue about their convictions and experiences? Their horizons widen to include the existence of wells other than their own. But they still have no suspicion of the existence of the ocean of truth that cannot be confined within the walls of conceptual wells. And our poor frogs continue to be divided and to speak in terms of yours and mine, your experience, your convictions, your ideology and mine. The sharing of formulas does not enrich the sharers, for formulas like the walls of wells divide; only the unrestricted ocean unites. But to arrive at this ocean of truth that is unbounded by formulas, it is essential to have the gift of clear thinking.

What is clear thinking and how does one arrive at it? The first thing you must know is that it does not call for any great learning. It is so simple as to be within the reach of a ten-year-old child. What is needed is not learning but unlearning, not talent but courage. You will understand this if you think of a little child in the arms of an old, disfigured housemaid. The child is too young to have picked up the prejudices of its elders. So when it snuggles in that woman's arms, it is responding not to labels in its head; labels like white woman, black woman, ugly, pretty, old, young, mother, servant maid, it is responding not to labels such as these but to reality. That woman meets the child's need for love and that is the reality the child responds to, not the woman's name and figure and religion and race and sect. Those are totally and absolutely irrelevant. The child has as yet no beliefs and no prejudices. This is the environment within which clear thinking can occur. And to achieve it one must drop everything one has learned and achieve the mind of the child that is innocent of past experiences and programming which so cloud our way of looking at reality.

Look into yourself and examine your reactions to persons and situations, and you will be appalled to discover the prejudiced thinking behind your reactions. It is almost never the concrete reality of this person or thing that you are responding to. You are responding to principles, ideologies, belief systems, economic, political, religious, psychological belief systems; to preconceived ideas and prejudices, whether positive or negative. Take them one at a time, each person and thing and situation and search for your bias separating the reality here before you from your programmed perceptions and your projections. And this exercise will afford you a revelation as divine as any that the Scriptures could provide you with.

Prejudices and beliefs are not the only enemies of clear thinking. There is another pair of enemies called desire and fear. Thinking that is uncontaminated by emotion, namely by desire and fear, and self-interest, calls for an asceticism that is terrifying. People mistakenly assume that their thinking is done by their head; it is done actually by the heart which first dictates the conclusion, then commands the head to provide the reasoning that will defend it. So here is another source of divine revelation. Examine some of the conclusions that you have arrived at and see how they are adulterated by self-interest. This is true of every conclusion, unless you hold it provisionally. Think how tightly you hold on to your conclusions regarding people, for instance. Are those judgments completely free of emotion? If you think they are, you have probably not looked hard enough.

This is the major cause of disagreements and

division between nations and individuals. Your interests do not coincide with mine, so your thinking and your conclusions do not agree with mine. How many people do you know whose thinking is at least sometimes opposed to their self-interest? How many times can you recall having engaged in that kind of thinking yourself? How often have you succeeded in placing an impenetrable barrier between the thinking going on in your head and the fears and desires that agitate your heart? Each time you attempt that task you will understand that what clear thinking calls for is not intelligence—that is easily come by—but the courage that has successfully coped with fear and with desire, for the moment you desire something or fear something, your heart will consciously or unconsciously get in the way of your thinking.

This is a consideration for spiritual giants who have come to realize that in order to find truth they need, not doctrinal formulations, but a heart that divests itself of its programming and its self-interest each time that thinking is in progress; a heart that has nothing to protect and owes nothing to ambition and therefore leaves the mind to roam unfettered, fearless and free, in search of truth; a heart that is ever ready to accept new evidence and to change its views. Such a heart then becomes a lamp that enlightens the darkness of the whole body of human-ity. If all human beings were fitted with such hearts people would no longer think of them-selves as communists or capitalists, as Christians or Muslims or Buddhists. The very clarity of their thinking would show them that all thinking, all concepts, all beliefs are lamps full of darkness, signs of their ignorance. And in that realization the walls of their separate wells would collapse and they would be invaded by the ocean that unites all peoples in the truth.

BE READY

‿

THEREFORE YOU ALSO MUST BE READY; FOR
THE SON OF MAN IS COMING AT AN HOUR
YOU DO NOT EXPECT.

—MATTHEW 24:44

Sooner or later there arises in every human
heart the desire for holiness, spirituality, God,
call it what you will. One hears mystics speak of
a divinity all around them that is within our
grasp, that would make our lives meaningful
and beautiful and rich, if we could only discover
it. People have some sort of a vague idea as to
what this thing is and they read books and con-
sult gurus, in the attempt to find out what it is
that they must do to gain this elusive thing
called Holiness or Spirituality. They pick up all
sorts of methods, techniques, spiritual exercises,
formulas; then after years of fruitless striving
they become discouraged and confused and
wonder what went wrong. Mostly they blame

143

themselves. If they had practiced their techniques more regularly, if they had been more
fervent or more generous, they might have made
it. But made what? They have no clear idea as to
what exactly this holiness that they seek is, but
they certainly know that their lives are still in a
mess, they still become anxious and insecure
and fearful, resentful and unforgiving, grasping
and ambitious and manipulative of people. So
once again they throw themselves with renewed
vigor into the effort and labor that they think
they need to attain their goal.

They have never stopped to consider this
simple fact: Their efforts are going to get them
nowhere. Their efforts will only make things
worse, as things become worse when you use
fire to put out fire. Effort does not lead to
growth; effort, whatever the form it may take,
whether it be willpower or habit or a technique
or a spiritual exercise, does not lead to change.
At best it leads to repression and a covering
over of the root disease.

Effort may change the behavior but it does
not change the person. Just think what kind of a
mentality it betrays when you ask, "What must
I do to get holiness?" Isn't it like asking, How
much money must I spend to buy something?
What sacrifice must I make? What discipline
must I undertake? What meditation must I prac-

tice in order to get it? Think of a man who wants to win the love of a woman and attempts to improve his appearance or build his body or change his behavior and practice techniques to charm her.

You truly win the love of others not by the practice of techniques but by being a certain kind of person. And that is never achieved through effort and techniques. And so it is with Spirituality and Holiness. Not what you do is what brings it to you. This is not a commodity that one can buy or a prize that one can win. What matters is what you are, what you become.

Holiness is not an achievement, it is a Grace. A Grace called Awareness, a grace called Looking, Observing, Understanding. If you would only switch on the light of awareness and observe yourself and everything around you throughout the day, if you would see yourself reflected in the mirror of awareness the way you see your face reflected in a looking glass, that is, accurately, clearly, exactly as it is without the slightest distortion or addition, and if you observed this reflection without any judgment or condemnation, you would experience all sorts of marvelous changes coming about in you. Only you will not be in control of those changes, or be able to plan them in advance, or decide how and when they are to take place. It is this nonjudgmental awareness alone that heals and changes and makes one grow. But in its own way and at its own time.

What specifically are you to be aware of? Your reactions and your relationships. Each time you are in the presence of a person, any person, or with Nature or with any particular situation, you have all sorts of reactions, positive and negative. Study those reactions, observe what exactly they are and where they come from, without any sermonizing or guilt or even any desire, much less effort to change them. That is all that one needs for holiness to arise.

But isn't awareness itself an effort? Not if you have tasted it even once. For then you will understand that awareness is a delight, the delight of a little child moving out in wonder to discover the world. For even when awareness uncovers unpleasant things in you, it always brings liberation and joy. Then you will know that the unaware life is not worth living, it is too full of darkness and pain.

If at first there is a sluggishness in practicing awareness, don't force yourself. That would be an effort again. Just be aware of your sluggishness without any judgment or condemnation. You will then understand that awareness involves as much effort as a lover makes to go to

∽

his beloved, or a hungry man makes to eat his food, or a mountaineer to get to the top of his beloved mountain; so much energy expended, so much hardship even, but it isn't effort, it's fun! In other words, awareness is an effortless activity.

Will awareness bring you the holiness you so desire? Yes and no. The fact is you will never know. For true holiness, the type that is not achieved through techniques and efforts and repression, true holiness is completely unselfconscious. You wouldn't have the slightest awareness of its existence in you. Besides you will not care, for even the ambition to be holy will have dropped as you live from moment to moment a life made full and happy and transparent through awareness. It is enough for you to be watchful and awake. For in this state your eyes will see the Savior. Nothing else, but absolutely nothing else. Not security, not love, not belonging, not beauty, not power, not holiness—nothing else will matter anymore.